I AM AN EXPERIMENT

An Extraordinary Spiritual Adventure

Ashtara's real life adventure story shows that life itself can often be stranger than fiction. If one reads this book with an open and non-judgmental mind then it has the ability to open doorways into a new reality that can offer an alternate explanation into the purpose of human existence. Ashtara has shown incredible bravery by sharing her inner journey with a world that describes all that is not seen by the eye as fantasy. By doing so her story will become a lifeboat to many who have experienced similar inner realities, and who have suffered torment when speaking of them to others.

Anyone who spends time with Ashtara will see that she is a very down-to-earth and practical woman who has been able to balance an extraordinary inner life with an outer life that has involved both business and community service. I believe this stability has enabled her to view these life experiences with the mindset and detachment of the scientist, being neither swayed nor overcome by the things she experienced. *I Am An Experiment* is a truthful documentation and unabridged version of these experiences.

This book will appeal to open minded seekers on the spiritual path. Many people will see the truth in Ashtara's telling of her life and will respond to her as a kindred spirit who has personally experienced and travelled through the unseen worlds documented in many of the ancient and archaic texts. Not all people will wish to consider that the information contained in this book could represent an undeveloped side of our human nature, however, it will certainly open the doorway for lively discussion and experimentation into it's possibilities. *I Am An Experiment* is an exciting and very informative read.

Lyndall White, B.A.H.Sc, M.A.Visual Art, Adv. Dip Homeopathy, Post Grad Psych.

I AM AN EXPERIMENT

An Extraordinary Spiritual Adventure

Ashtara

Published by Tara Rising in 2013
P.O Box 640
Nerang, QLD 4211 Australia
www.IAmAnExperiment.com

Copyright © 2012 Ashtara

Catalogue-in-Publication details available on request
from the National Library of Australia.

ISBN: 978-0-9876007-0-7 (pbk)

Also available as an ebook
ebook ISBN: 978-0-9876007-1-4

All rights reserved. No part of this book may be reproduced or transmitted in any form or by any means, electronic or mechanical, without written permission from the author or publisher except for quotations embodied in critical articles or reviews.

Cover design: In2Art Designs

Book design and publishing assistance by
Publicious P/L
www.publicious.com.au

Also written by Ashtara
Gaia, Our Precious Planet
Tara, Emissary of Light
The Great Cosmic Joke
A Treasure Trove of Gems
A Crack in the Cosmic Window
Your Recipe for Empowerment through Spiritual Astrology
Volumes One, Two and Three
Esoteric Astrology, The Astrology of the Soul

DEDICATION

This book is dedicated to my son, Andrew, and his family in USA who provided a nurturing and loving home environment that enabled me to recuperate from a debilitating illness.

I wrote the first draft of this book in Copacabana, a small fishing village on the shores of Lake Titicaca, Bolivia, a country I loved and had visited each year for nine years. I intended to stay for six week to write this book but, five hours after completing the first draft, I suddenly became very ill. Three days later I had to leave to travel by bus to the capitol La Paz to find a flight out of the country. I had only been in Copacabana six days. Andrew, you and your family were there for me when I reached USA and I thank you from the bottom of my heart for your hospitality, consideration and loving care.

I love you all so much.

CONTENTS

ACKNOWLEDGEMENTS......................i
INTRODUCTION................................iii

PART ONE
1993 & 1994 - AN AWAKENING....Page 1

The Quest, Christian Upbringing, An Awakening at Santa Fe, Chiron Return, Introduction to Spiritual Guides: 1993 - Astrology and Sound Training, Esoteric Psychology, The Woman of Luminosity, 1994 – Inter-dimensional Experiences, Crystal Healing, Crystal Technology, The Writing Process, Introduction to Sai Baba, White Buffalo Woman, The Sacred Circle Dance, Paneurythmy; A Scientific Experiment, The Council of Nine.

PART TWO
1995 - DEDICATION TO THE LIGHT.....Page 41

The Sacred Journey, Gaia's Ascension, Colour Therapy, Zeolite, The Obelisk, The Archangel Michael, Dedication to the Light, Understanding of Creation, An Important Lesson, A Cosmic Identity, Mr Squiggle, Independence, A Pleiadian Experiment, A Repeat Experiment, Hidden Symbols, Transmission of Love, The Archangels Wings, A Bulgarian Adventure, Spiritual Growth Accelerates, Zodiacal Polarities, Supreme Being, Pleiadian Message, Optimum Health, The Role of Light Beings, Pegasus, the Cosmic Horse, The Structure and Form of Creation.

PART THREE
1996, 1997 & 1998 - HISTORY REVEALED.....Page 99

The Comet, The Spiritual Hierarchy, A Space Craft, Meeting with Jesus/Sananda, Saturn and Chiron, The Path of Self-Love, Universal Design Patterns, Speaking the Truth, A Treasure Chest, Gaia's Pain, The Sirian Connection, USA Astrology Conference, Galactic Council Meeting, The Seven Sisters, My Soul's History, The Higher Self, The Lords of Orion, A Precious Accolade, Book Launch, Australian Walk-About, The White Buffalo, Rearrangement of Molecules, The Sirian Temple of Light.

PART FOUR
1999 - A PRIESTESS OF ISIS.....Page 138

Sirian Beings Revealed, The Star, Gaia's Heartbeat, Abraham's Message, Mary Magdalen, Intuitive Words, A Title Remembered, Discrimination, Forgiveness, Ashtara, A Priestess of Isis, An Ending, Introduction to Antares, Ascended Master Lord Kuthumi.

PART FIVE
2000 - A NEW MILLENNIUM & IDENTITY.....Page 172

A new Millennium, The Dragon, Ancient Wisdom with a New Look, The Comet's Message, Antares Training, Arcturus, Further Antares Training, Celestial Neon Colours, Departure of 1D and 2D Elementals, A Jupiter/Uranus Experience, Perturbation into Greater Light, Farewell to Antares, I Am You and You Are Me, A Record Keeper, South America, Gestation of The Golden Age, Training by the Spiritual Hierarchy, Perception, Frequencies of Energy, Energetic Density, Preparing to Fly, USA Adventure, A "Walk-In" Experience.

ACKNOWLEDGEMENTS

This book could not have been written without the main characters. The list is long and you will read about them in this book. They are living light beings operating in higher dimensions to that of humans. For many years they were my trainers and I will be eternally grateful for their love, teaching and healing. The experiences I had with them were real, and their method of training was experiential, persistent and remarkable.

I wish to thank my beloved daughters, Catherine and Christine, who provided chiropractic treatments when my right hip and knee became troublesome during the writing of my story. My friends Ruth Robson and Alison Downes, through their amazing healing treatments, enabled me to source, and overcome, my fear of publishing this book and I sincerely thank them for their caring expertise.

A graphic artist friend, Joan Ellerby, created the initial design for the cover image and, when it was inadvertently destroyed, another friend, Carolyn Gibson, stepped in to help me create a new, similar one. Thank you Carolyn for your support, not only for your technological expertise but also for your consideration, love and care. Your faith in me provided the encouragement I needed to continue writing my story. Rose Allan, my editor, through her continual requests to "explain" and "what do you mean", encouraged me to turn this book into one more user friendly. Thank you so much Rose. I know the content was a stretch for you.

With sincere gratitude I acknowledge my Bolivian friend and tour guide Rosse Mary Vargas. Without her loving support I may not be here now, nor would this book be written. Her efficient organisation enabled me to spend my last few days in Bolivia in a safe and energetically clean five-star hotel in La Paz. She also organized the needed changes to my flights that enabled me to travel to USA to recuperate, with my son and his family, from a debilitating illness contacted a few hours after the completion of the first draft of this book. You will always be very dear to my heart RosseMary.

I feel so blessed and fortunate to have such a wonderful support team and I love you all. Thank you so much.

INTRODUCTION

"Through all-seeing Mind, I myself have been the witness of the invisible things of Heaven, and through contemplation come to the knowledge of the Truth. This knowing I have set down in these writing...."
Hermes/Thoth

This book is my personal story. One of memoirs, recorded in my daily journal between 1993 and 2000. It is an extraordinary adventure into unknown dimensional realms. My experiences arose from dedicated spiritual aspiration, disciplined daily meditation and regular spiritual practices. The story details my ascension into realms of celestial light and ecstatic divine love.

During my daily meditation practice celestial and extra-terrestrial beings trained me to 'remote view'. Remote viewing is the ability to mind travel to an intentional location to view places, events, people and things. NASA trains people to do this. I was also taught to communicate telepathically and to bi-locate i.e. to use all six senses and experience full bodily sensations while operating in multi-dimensional localities. Most of my training involved navigating celestial realms and meeting, identifying and inter-acting with the highly evolved light-beings residing there. They taught me to awaken within my mind and body different frequency ranges. The training processes were fun. My trainers were incredibly loving and considerate, and the processes felt familiar and natural, as if I'd experienced them before, in another time.

Very early in the training I realized that my consciousness could travel to areas my rational mind couldn't access. My trainers asked that I record my experiences and share them at the appropriate time. That time is now.

My work is to awaken and catalyse people into the understanding and experience of broader realities and of the infinite nature of consciousness and divine love. I am dedicated to my work.

The content of this book is true for me. It is for you to ascertain its truth through your intuition and heart-felt response.

I invite you to fasten your seat belts and travel with me into unchartered starry realms.

    Ashtara
    November 2012

PART ONE

AN AWAKENING

The Quest

I was determined to transform my life and used to go on my early morning walks thumping my thymus and affirming "I am willing to change" "I am willing to change". I felt this affirmation profoundly. I meant it.

Why did I begin this spiritual quest? Simple answer: depression. My 'wake-up' call came in 1987, around the time of the Harmonic Convergence, when many thousands of people globally united in groups to pray for world peace.

Why was I suffering such deep depression? It didn't make sense. Externally I had all the trappings of success: a beautiful home and thriving business, three wonderful children and financial security. Internally my soul was crying out with a hunger for something, yet I knew not what.

It was time to change, but change what? I felt I was in a giant mental fog with confusion part of the depression. Who was I when not playing the supportive, nurturing role to husband, children, dog and business? I never considered visiting a doctor to fix my problem because I had realized, many years earlier, that drugs were detrimental to my sensitive energy system. I nearly died when I was twenty-four, by being given too much anaesthetic, and wasn't willing to put myself through that experience again.

In early 1988 one of my daughters gave me the gift of a week's retreat at a health camp. I enjoyed the week immensely and, through active participation in the courses, learned much about myself. Part of the program was to assist people clear blocked emotions. This was the first time I had experienced psychological work and had no frame of reference to understand it. All my life I'd stuffed my emotions down thus unwittingly displaying a false façade. I did not know how to identify any specific emotion I felt, let alone verbalize it. I went back to this Health Retreat three times and, on the third, one of the guest speakers spoke about astrology. My sceptical mind stood guard.

I had not known of the world of astrology before, so was wary. However something inside of me resonated with the way the speaker, Christopher Power, presented the subject. A tiny spark of curiosity ignited an uplifting feeling in my heart and I decided to follow it. I visited Christopher for an astrological reading and, when invited to sit down at his desk, crossed my arms over my chest and refused to speak other than give him my birth particulars. This was all the information he needed.

To my surprise he told me what I was currently experiencing emotionally, and in particular the depression. And he gave me a great gift - the psychological tools to enable me to overcome it. He explained how my subconscious emotions could be likened to a reservoir overflowing beyond capacity, and how the reservoir wall was crumbling due to the amount and weight of the 'water' in it. My supressed emotions were the 'water'. He said the current planetary movements connecting to my horoscope were the activating agents for the emotional 'flooding' and how important it was for the emotions to be released. He taped the consultation and I went home armed with my first astrological/psychological tools, feeling incredibly grateful for the experience.

I found the language difficult to understand because the concepts were totally foreign. I was used to business language. However I persisted, transcribing the tape to paper and carrying the document with me wherever I went. Each evening I reviewed it, endeavouring to gain greater understanding. I worked in my business from 8.30am until 4.30pm, six days a week, and my husband worked in it from 4.30 until 10.00pm so I had plenty of time in the evenings to study, and integrate the astrological information.

I decided to apply this information to my daily life. What did I have to lose? I felt I had been given the opportunity to open my mind to a completely new way of thinking and being. I was learning about myself and this was something I had never considered because my focus had always been on supporting and caring for others. I didn't know who I was underneath the devoted wife and mother, social organizer or businesswoman roles.

By the end of the year I felt lighter and more alive. I wasn't depressed any more. I knew astrology worked, because I experienced major regeneration, not only physically but also mentally and emotionally. Astrology enabled me to identify, accept and face my inner demons, take responsibility for them and act upon transforming them – daily. I felt it was manna from heaven. I requested another reading and the internal investigative processes began again, however this time there were different psychological themes and issues to understand and work through. The astrologer said this was because some of the travelling planets had moved on from their former activations to specific placements in my birth chart. I had apparently worked through the top layers of deeply entrenched psychological issues so they faded away. This former sceptic became a strong believer in the ancient science and art of astrology, and how it could be used as an empowering self-healing tool.

Christian Upbringing

I was brought up in an Anglo-Saxon protestant household and taken to Sunday school when I was five years old. I loved the church, the teachings and the singing of hymns. My life outside home and school involved the church. When I was around seven years old I had a confrontation with a catholic priest who was visiting the next-door neighbour. I overheard the priest telling the neighbour that God was to be feared. I was resolute that God was love and that it was wicked to say otherwise, so I said so. I received a violent and judgemental re-action from the priest.

So I started studying the Bible and would often be found reading alone, in the cold lounge room, filling myself with the scriptures. I remember often play-acting my dream scene for adulthood. This was to teach the truth of Jesus teachings, not in a building, but in nature. The only way I could imagine how this could happen was to become a teaching missionary in Africa.

My sporting activities and the annual camping

expeditions to the mountains were an essential part of the church programmes. I regularly taught Sunday school, read lessons in the pulpit and sang my heart out in the church services until someone cautioned me to be quiet, saying I had a terrible voice. This shut me up, for many years. I married in this church then left Australia to live in Fiji, an island country. There were no Anglo-Saxon churches nearby so I conducted my own Easter and Christmas services at home, alone.

After spending nearly five years on this idyllic island paradise we, my husband, two children and I, returned to Australia to live. I hoped there would be a church in the remote western Tasmanian area where we were to live. And there was.

I attended this church on two or three occasions and then began receiving home visits from the minister. On one of these visits he tried to sexually molest me. That was the end of my church life. All my naïve and innocent beliefs regarding the behaviour of God's so called representatives were smashed. A huge black hole developed in my heart and soul that lasted for twenty-four years.

Those years were filled with family life, business and material pursuits. During my mid to late forties I began to experience extremes of emotional intensity and ill health. It was wake-up time yet I had no idea what I was to 'wake-up' to.

An Awakening at Santa Fe

I'd had enough of trade shows. I'd participated in so many during the past fifteen years of jewellery business life. My husband, who bought all the precious gem stones for our business, planned to attend the annual jewellery and gem stone trade show in Denver, Colorado USA and invited me to go with him. But I needed a change, a new look at life. Finding a seven-day retreat workshop in Santa Fe at the exact time of the show I booked my place and a seat on the small plane from Denver. The workshop was held in an old monastery, built in the early 1600's. It felt wonderful to have my own room, even though it was only for a week, and to be part of the history of the area. I loved Santa Fe and the venue. What magic and mystery would unfold here? I wondered.

Plenty. The facilitator had lived and trained with Native American Indians for more than twenty years and much of the weeks' training was based upon their mind-expanding methods to enable the raising of consciousness. At this early stage of my spiritual journey I had no idea what consciousness meant. On the first morning we played games that connected us with nature and I enjoyed them so much. They were fun, easy and stimulating. However the other students appeared to find them exceedingly challenging. Later in the morning the facilitator asked me not to play again because I apparently knew the games so well. How come? I thought. This same response continued with each exercise throughout that day and the next.

On the third day we were asked to meditate and then, immediately afterwards, gather in a circle for a special exercise. Meditation was easy for me. I'd only been practicing regularly for maybe a year but seemed to enter an altered state of mind quickly. I also realized I created a tremendous amount of heat in my body when I totally focused and relaxed into the process.

I chose to meditate lying on the floor and created heat and light in my body through deep, slow, focused breathing. I could feel my body and hands tingling with energy currents. Then, when instructed, we silently grouped into a circle, sat on chairs, and were each given a heavy silver dessertspoon. We were asked to stroke the handle and bend it. This will be easy, I thought. I'd seen a Russian man do this same exercise on a TV show and people had marvelled at him however I knew all it required was focus and belief. I stroked the handle and within seconds the heavy metal softened and bent, doubling over itself. I showed it to the facilitator who promptly and silently gave me another one to bend, which I did equally as easily.

All the other students looked at the bent spoons with amazement. There were only two people who were then able to bend their spoons. It was following this game I found out the other students were psychologists and had come to this retreat from many different countries. When I booked my place I hadn't realized it was a specialised training programme designed to expand the consciousness of psychologists. Whoops! What was I doing here?

On the next day we began training to expand and enhance our peripheral vision. This meant developing the ability to see beyond normal vision boundaries. This specific training took all day. Many interesting exercises were undertaken and again I didn't take them very seriously. I was so enjoying my playtime. In the evening, following our long practice, we were driven into the desert. The exercise given was to take turns in leading the others back to the truck after we had walked a long distance to a specific area. We were told there would not be any moonlight and that the only light would come from the stars. We were not permitted to use flashlights.

Before we began our early evening walk, and while

it was still light, we were asked to concentrate on the vegetation and use it as guideposts for our return. As we walked the two and a half-hour journey to the point of the return trip I found myself unable to do as requested. Instead I became immersed in coyote calls and the beauty of nature. I smelt the desert and sensed a connection to the land. It was different to that of Australia yet I felt at home. Before we embarked upon the return journey we were allocated our times for individual leadership. I was to be last.

I enjoyed being in the wide-open spaces and, when it was my turn to lead, I intuitively closed my eyes and a path immediately appeared in my inner vision. It was very clear. I confidently walked this path, gathering momentum with each step. I led the group for approximately twenty-five minutes and then my vision vanished. I instantly stopped. The facilitator, who, unbeknown to me, had walked directly behind came and stood beside me and showed, with his flashlight, where we were. I could see the truck down below on the flat. He said I had led the group along a very old cow trail that he hadn't seen or walked before. He seemed surprised. I felt elated because the whole process felt natural, as if I'd done it many times before.

On our return to the truck we were invited to play the available instruments. I chose a Native American drum, never having seen, or played one before. The drum was light and easy to carry and appeared to be made from an animal hide stretched tightly over a round solid frame. The frame extended to a hand-grip. I held the instrument in my left hand and my right hand and fingers appeared to have a life of their own creating a rhythm that my body immediately responded to. I was feeling incredibly exhilarated and drummed freely for two hours without stopping. I danced as I drummed, enjoying myself immensely. I felt I was in a familiar time and place, completely connected to the land. I love to dance and did so with gay abandon.

The final day of the retreat was strange and unsettling. We were asked to create two teams by first scanning the room and then standing on the side of the room where we felt the most comfortable. I spent some time choosing my place because I somehow knew it was an important part of the exercise. After I did so others, mostly women, gathered to stand beside me. We then sat down in two rows facing each other. There were approximately ten people in each team. The game to be played was a competition with the scores being kept by an assistant, using two ropes. A knot would be tied in the appropriate rope when one of the teams scored a point.

The facilitator walked in front of each team player, one team at a time, holding three stones in one of his closed hands. He offered his two fists to each member who had to intuitively select the hand that held the stones. Once the game was explained I immediately knew how to play it. First our team members were to distract the other team to prevent them from intuiting the correct hand. This was easy to do. We were mostly women and played our femininity to the hilt. It was fun and exhilarating. We were able to intuit correctly and we were winning.

After a number of games the facilitator called for a break. We were asked to group into our teams at each end of the room and he came to speak with our group first, with a special request. This was for us to enable the other team to win. He said we knew we had won anyway and there was no need to go any further. We agreed, accepting and respecting his request. I didn't think about the reason behind his action nor was it discussed.

The game resumed. We remained quiet and allowed the other team to win. However this was not a good idea. Some of the men from the other team became so angry they punched two of the women on our side, stormed off and left the programme to return home, hours before it was due to end. I was amazed, and saddened by the behaviour of these professionals.

Only many years later did I realize where and how I had developed the skills I'd demonstrated at the conference. I had learned them well in another lifetime and the memories of that time came to me as feelings and intuitive knowing. My conscious rational mind had no understanding of the process.

As a result of this wonderful experience of remembrance, and at the suggestion of the facilitator, upon my return home to Australia I learned the ancient Japanese hands-on healing art of Reiki and from then worked with it for self-healing and healing others. It seemed natural and easy. I also attended a workshop given by a North American Indian who taught drum making. I made my own drum.

Chiron Return

And then it was time for my 'Chiron Return'. This is an astrological cycle that happens to everyone around the ages of 49 - 51. The planets in our solar system orbit the Sun in time cycles. Chiron's cycle is approximately 50 years. Chiron is not officially designated a planet however people experience its energetic influence, usually unconsciously.

It is when Chiron returns to its birth chart position that subconscious soul wounds emerge that require self-awareness in order for them to heal. These wounds may be physical but have a psychological foundation. Life changing events can also take place around this age.

At my Chiron return I sought medical help even though I hardly ever visited doctors. I had a very strong constitution and was usually very healthy. However, my tummy extended to such an extent it appeared I was nine months pregnant. I walked bent over, as if very old. I was diagnosed as anaemic and iron deficient. Now I understand that the cause of my belly swelling was due to holding in emotions all my life. The fluid from this suppression extended my stomach to that huge extent.

During this time my eldest daughter gave me a book *Spiritual Astrology* by Jan Spiller and Karen McCoy. This book became my bible, lifeline and salvation. I worked intensely on myself with it, especially the section on the pre-natal eclipses, and gradually began to turn my life around.

Everyone's journey to self-discovery, self-understanding and acceptance is different and this was the path shown for me to follow. I loved astrology and the amazing results I was experiencing through applying the teachings to myself, and I wanted to learn as much as I could. So I gave my husband a year's notice from our business. I offered to give the business to him if he wanted to run it himself. However he chose not to. I wasn't sure how I would manage my material world but I knew that what I was doing was no longer working, and my health would suffer if I didn't make the change.

At the conclusion of that year I closed down the business, sold most of the stock and ended an 18.5-

year (an astrological nodal cycle) chapter of my life. My husband was now at a loose end and concerned about what he would do with his working life. He was a Mining Engineer and Gemmologist so had many options.

Going back to school and commencing formal study of astrology was a stretch, however I felt I had come home to myself. This was definitely where I needed, and wanted, to be. All that was being taught by my amazing astrology teacher, Maggie Kerr, felt so right, as if it was something I was dredging up, that I'd known and practised before in my soul's history. I realized I had a great deal to learn and had only touched the surface of this ancient sacred science. I attended one class per week for the first year and then two classes weekly for the second and third years. I worked daily on my study, applying every new concept to my personal life. It was a time of huge transformation, intense psychological self-analysis, healing and truth finding.

1993 - Introduction to Spiritual Guides

Shadrack.

The name sounded familiar. Where had I heard it before? I wanted an answer to the strange repetitive experiences occurring every night I drifted off to sleep. I'd become aware of the sound of a cassette tape turning on and, as I awakened the next morning, turning off in my head. I wanted to know who was operating this tape and what information was being subliminally downloaded. So I mentally asked.

Much to my surprise I received an immediate one-word reply. Shadrack. A rusty cog in the wheel of my mind activated. What information did the tape contain? Why was Shadrack feeding it to me? Who was he? I needed to find out more.

So I phoned a friend who was able to direct me to a chapter in the Bible to source Shadrack. He was one of the three wise men (astrologers) called to the court of Nebuchadnezzar to interpret his dreams. I have two Bibles in my home. One is an old King James edition, and the other a Presbyterian one given to my grandmother in 1908 on the occasion of her marriage. I delved into the King James translation, Book of Daniel, chapter two, and found Shadrack mentioned. I also found the words astrology and astrologers mentioned thirteen times. However, when I checked my family Bible the astrology words had been omitted. This made me aware that the bible information I was fed as a child was contaminated and determined by the consciousness of the translator. This was a shock.

I didn't dwell upon it. I was so excited to find the information on Shadrack because I realized he was teaching me astrology in my sleep. I felt very fortunate indeed.

In the beginning of my astrological training I found it difficult to embrace symbolism because I had been brought up to believe that all I was taught, especially from the Bible, was the literal truth. I learned that symbols contain profound expressions of human nature and have been used in all cultures down through the astrological Ages of time. One symbol contains a large package of specific information. Astrology decodes the information 'packages' contained within each astrological symbol. I needed to make a 180 - degree mental shift to integrate this new concept. I also found it difficult to understand the detailed astronomy part of the course. But I learned, and integrated easily, the broader concepts and the psychological teaching. The serious and determined application of astrology to my life enabled me to consciously identify, accept and then change old self-destructive psychological patterning. I am so grateful for the teaching I received.

While studying astrology I also studied metaphysics, esoteric science and spiritual principles and practices. To me astrology and spirituality are intimately connected. I devoured spiritual books as if they were soul food. It was as if I intuitively knew I'd found the keys I needed to access deeply rooted psychological problems and heal myself. The dark hole within my soul slowly began to fill with light, the light of higher consciousness. I combined my spiritual, metaphysical, esoteric and astrological training into a philosophical package that worked for me.

During this time my husband and I were having relationship problems. He couldn't understand the path I was taking and I didn't have the language to explain it in the scientific terms he needed. Each day when psychological issues arose in our relationship I chose to accept responsibility for everything I was feeling. I worked on identifying my emotions, feelings and body sensations until I understood their truth. I was willing to be my own 'guinea pig' applying everything I learned to myself. I knew that I would not know how astrology worked unless I experienced the positive effects of working through my psychological issues, clearly indicated in each astrological symbol in my birth chart. I reasoned it would only be intellectual information if it stayed in my head.

I sometimes felt as if I was inside a pressure cooker. Unprocessed emotions from aeons of times past, stored in my cellular memory, began to surface. I understood them to be unprocessed past-life issues that required resolution this time around. I learnt to feel, and differentiate between, the transiting planetary energies in my mind and body. I also learned that, at specific astrological times, the cosmic energies activate deep soul memories. These memories were of my soul's journey not only here on planet Earth but also in other dimensions of time and space. I learned astrology well. It became obvious to me that I had previously learned and worked with astrology in another life.

Since then I have healed myself from all health problems although sometimes I had to be assisted by alternate healers when I wasn't able to access psychological cause.

I learned that negative beliefs are like weeds in a garden. Some patterns are very deeply rooted and need extra time and effort to extract them from their well-lodged, brain washed position. These weeds need constant attention for they lower one's vibratory level and create a great deal of emotional angst.

Astrology and Sound Training

I became a workshop junkie. One of the things I learned, very early in my spiritual training, was to be very discriminating with teachers. I was only willing to learn from those who came from their heart, as opposed to their ego. I would sit in the class, workshop or meditation group and focus my attention on my heart felt feelings and bodily sensations. If I felt the teacher was coming from their heart then I would continue. If not, I was out of there. I wanted genuine, sincere, heart-felt wisdom, learned from years of experience, not information from pumped-up self-acclaimed gurus who believed they were the greatest gift to humankind.

As well as my weekly classes I also attended astrological conferences, seminars and workshops desiring to learn as much as I could from a variety of teachers. One session changed my life forever. The group was led into three different creative visualization meditations and the experiences I had were profound. One of the guided processes was to take a journey into a nurturing forest and then rest on a mat, admiring the beauty of nature. We were then asked to mentally create an image of our personal birth chart emerging into the space in front of our resting place. The next step was to imagine walking into the centre of our birth chart. From that centre we were asked to invoke specific planets.

This was an extraordinary experience, one that became more relevant as the years passed by. This meditation into my birth chart became one of my regular practices because I used it to easily identify and resolve psycho-spiritual issues. I still use the process whenever I need to. It by passes the logical mind and allows one's intuitive wisdom to speak. I learned to know all the planets on a personal basis and it wasn't long before they acted as spiritual guides and cosmic jokers. I realized they are archetypal forces within our psyche that can be cajoled, loved, worked with and with a bit of effort, managed. I created two CDs an *Inner Home* meditation and *Invoking the Planets* so others could experience similar transformative processes.

Also during the early years of formal astrological training I attended many spiritual growth workshops. One was an intense one-week residential sound and voice training. I was determined to heal the belief that I had a terrible voice. My experiences had shown that changing the mind is one thing, but to integrate and fully embody the change takes a lot more inner work. I could affirm that I had a beautiful voice two hundred times a day but it didn't alter the fact that I didn't. I totally believed that everyone has access to a beautiful voice and was determined to find mine.

During the workshop a past life emerged into my consciousness. It was one in which I had my throat deliberately cut because I was about to reveal powerful information that would bring a great deal of illumination to others. This wasn't allowed, hence my early death. I was able to access and clear the energetic psychological residue residing in my throat chakra, one of the seven main energy centres in the body, and this left me feeling much lighter. I toned special sounds to aid the healing process.

After this process I became aware of a beautiful clear and bright royal blue light around my head and throat. It felt and looked sensational so I asked the facilitator what it meant. He said I had obviously healed ancient baggage that had been stored in my throat chakra and was now accessing a spiritual guide. He suggested I ask who it was. I did, and had an immediate response. The name given this time was Joseph of Arimathea. Huh? Who was this? I thought. The teacher told me that Joseph of Arimathea was Jesus' uncle and a great supporter of his spiritual work. I felt humbled with this revelation and wondered why he was working with me.

So now I had the conscious understanding and the names of two spiritual guides. How many more were there?

During these early spiritual growth years I also spent regular weekly healing sessions undergoing past life regression and re-birthing processes. I was determined to access, clear and heal as much ancient dross from my subconscious as possible. I understood the purpose behind accessing past lives was to identify the cause of the psychological baggage created in the past that was perpetuating current self-sabotage. Once the meaning was clear I was able to transmute the negative energy into light.

I did this by relaxing my mind and body through meditation and deep breathing and then generating within my heart genuine feelings of love. And also by invoking radiant light rays to enter all my cells through my crown chakra. I focused on imagining and feeling the forces of love and light dissolving dense psychological patterning. I realized the importance of combining feeling and emotion with mind and body to enable holistic healing. I practiced sincere forgiveness on all who I perceived had harmed me. And then I forgave myself for unconsciously attracting the hardship.

I learned that fear is the slowest and most dense vibration and love is the highest. Fear ages and paralyses a body. Love regenerates a body. The story of the past life is irrelevant. It is the theme and psychological issue contained within the story and carried into this life that is important to resolve this time around. This process of transmutation of psychological density enables the cells to regenerate and youth, and the light of higher consciousness and divine love to permeate one's being. It is an alchemical process. The clarity and light shining in the eyes, the window of the soul, demonstrates the quality of consciousness (light) in each person.

The reason this specific past life experience came up was because I found it incredibly difficult to speak to my husband about my innermost feelings and truth. My fear of his reactions was so great. Following this workshop I was able to share my deepest feelings with him and this improved our relationship. My singing voice improved dramatically and I could now sing in tune.

On an intuitive level I understood that any dark, dense psychological baggage would eventually eat into my cells, lower my frequency and create serious illness later on in life. My goal at the time was to become as clean a channel for divinity as I could. I didn't want old dross and baggage to block my connections to lighter and higher dimensions of experience. I did my best to accomplish what I set out to do. That spiritual goal continues to this day.

At the end of the year I was offered the opportunity to sit for the first of many astrology exams. My teacher encouraged me to take the technical exam first. I agreed and prepared for it well. However it was a traumatic experience. Paralysing fear emerged as soon as I sat down to write the exam paper. I was terrified of making a mistake. On the completion of the exam I had to be helped out of the room because I was unable to walk. My spine felt frozen and my knees were so weak they couldn't carry me. I understood then that I carried, in my soul's memory banks, a past life experience directly related to technical astrology that connected to the fear. The last time I'd sat for an exam was when I was fifteen years old.

Esoteric Psychology

In 1994, when I began my second year of astrological studies, I decided to also study esoteric psychology. I had also been asked by my astrology teacher to be her co-teacher for the beginner's class. My days were filled with astrology, which, I believe, is the greatest tool to aid spiritual growth and enable optimum health. I continued applying everything I learned to myself to make sure it worked. It did - amazingly.

The esoteric psychology classes turned out to be advanced meditations. I am eternally grateful to my teacher because, by participating fully in the meditations, I learned to commune easily with other spiritual guides and to experience my totem animals. I also learned how to cleanse and purify my chakras. To my delight I was told I was a natural healer.

It was around this time I was asked by friends to share my knowledge and healing skills. I resisted because I didn't believe I knew enough, or felt confident enough. However, when more and more people asked for help and guidance I relented, on the proviso that I could only share what I had learned and nothing else and, if this was valuable then I was happy to do so.

I also learned to interpret my dreams and work with the Tarot, Numerology and the Moon's cycles and phases. And I was learning to develop and value my intuition.

The Woman of Luminosity

A woman emerged from the ethers
A smile dancing on her lips
Her skin was luminous, ethereal,
Who was she?
Was she from another time or another dimension?
As the mists of time dissolved
The face of the woman became clear,
And sparkled with luminosity
A heart shaped ring of red flowers encircled her head
She had a presence, a quality

Divine love emanating from her being
Who was She?
Where did she come from?
Was she from another time or another dimension?
Was she Venus, Aphrodite?
A woman emerged from the ethers
A smile dancing on her lips
Her skin was luminous, ethereal,
Her eyes were pools of endless light.
Her robe was silver, floating around her body
Giving her an air of softness and delicacy.
Who was She?
Where did she come from?
Was she from another time or another dimension?
"Can you enlighten me?" I ask,
"Are you an aspect of me?
Are you a representation of my Higher Self"?
Will the answer come?
The woman of luminosity asked that I travel with her
into her world to discover her secrets and message.
One dimension merged into another as we
joined together in the universal dance.
The woman of luminosity and I were one.

1994 - Inter-dimensional Experiences

I often wondered why human beings only used 10-15% of their brain capacity when there was another 85-90% still available to be utilized. I intuited that the rational left-brain couldn't provide the answer. We could fill our minds with information and put it into large mental filing cabinets but it wouldn't expand our brain capacity. The expansiveness needed to come through the intuitive and conceptual right brain that is connected to feeling and soul knowing. In the astrological model I understand this is through the Sagittarius channel. Gemini, its opposite sign, connects to the left-brain. I was open to the experience of right-brain expansion that I somehow knew could only come about during relaxation and meditation.

In a meditation early this year I was introduced to an eagle guide who invited me to travel with him into different dimensional realities. This was an expansive leap for me, however it seemed natural and familiar, so I chose to go along with it. I felt completely safe, fully trusting the process.

During one of these easy, and very enjoyable, space rides I was taken to a City of Light and brought before the Galactic Council. I was asked if I would perform a task for the Council as their emissary. It felt right in my heart and soul, so I agreed. I was told it was to do with bringing balance to the masculine and feminine energies on our planet so they could relate better. When I came out of the meditation, which I did easily, I questioned myself: What was a City of Light and who were the Galactic Council? I had no frame of reference and I didn't write any other details in my journal. I didn't understand the task given either, however I completely trusted I would when the time was right.

Approximately one month later, during another meditation, I was again taken, by my eagle guide, on a journey through space to meet a group of ten spiritual Masters. Each one said they had a special quality to teach me. These qualities were: intelligence, understanding, discernment, love, wisdom, beauty, compassion, humility and two more I didn't record. These spiritual guides continued to work with me for some time. I realized they did this by providing situations and events in my everyday world that enabled me to naturally develop these positive qualities. Usually the experiences were challenging, and I had to release many former beliefs in order to progress.

Another month later, and during my daily morning meditation, I was introduced to a new guide, Mary. She said she was going to help me embody the divine feminine. I didn't fully understand what this meant, nor did I know who this Mary was, but trusted I would find out. I felt she could have been Mother Mary but then doubted myself. Around the same time Lord Chohan, an ascended spiritual master, came into my meditative consciousness. Who was he? I asked myself.

My curiosity became aroused by these alternate reality experiences so I began reading specific spiritual books to find answers to my questions. I soon became aware of unseen forces guiding me to the right stores where the books containing the information I needed were sold.

I learned that an ascended spiritual master is a former human being who, while living on Earth, was dedicated to his or her spiritual growth path and willingly did the inner housekeeping necessary to purify psychological baggage. During the inner cleansing process many spiritual initiations took place. When the student was deemed to have developed, within their cells, sufficient spiritual light and love they were admitted into Mystery Schools or Ashrams that operated in higher dimensions, or frequency bands, where they were taught by highly evolved spirit guides.

Jesus and the Buddha are two well known ascended masters. Lord Chohan is obviously another. During another meditation he took me to the Council of Elders where I was asked to take part in an initiation ceremony. I was initiated into the Great White Brotherhood and given a charge - to work for humanity by serving myself first and then serving others as myself.

I was baptized into this Brotherhood of Spiritual Light and invited to call upon them when needed. The spokesperson said that, now I was one of their members, I had a responsibility and sacred trust. At some time in the future, I would be called upon to fulfil a special task. A mission. Until then I was to demonstrate integrity and honesty at all times.

At the conclusion of this meditation I researched the Great White Brotherhood and did my best to understand my charge. I discovered that the word "Chohan" is a title given by Buddhists to describe an enlightened being, an ascended Spiritual Master. The Great White Brotherhood is the name given to a highly evolved group of spiritual beings intent upon assisting humanity to evolve into the light of God/Christ or cosmic consciousness. "White" means spiritualized light.

The human spiritual evolutionary process is called ascension and the Great White Brotherhood is a branch of the Creator's Spiritual Hierarchy. Its membership consists of Angelic and cosmic beings. These light beings operate on higher frequency wave bands, or dimensions, to that of humans and are dedicated to serve the Prime Creator's Plan. The Great White Brotherhood can be likened to the organizational structure of a large business firm where the conditions of employment are dependant upon the attributes and qualities of the employee.

I intuitively understood that the charge I was given meant that my service to myself was to continue embodying greater spiritual love and light to enable the development of higher consciousness. It was by identifying, accepting, owning and loving every negative thought and emotion for its' teaching that I was able to infuse myself with spiritualised love and higher consciousness.

I learned to be the objective observer of myself feeling, thinking and acting. I serve others as myself by teaching those who want to learn from me how to do the same. Spiritual astrology, numerology and the tarot were the tools I chose. I very much enjoy this game of life.

My meditation experiences into other worlds seemed natural and right. When I came out of the harmonious, and usually blissful, states I wrote about the experiences in my daily journal as my guides asked me to do. The high frequency of love developed during the meditations stayed with me for some time afterwards and I became aware that my cellular structure was gradually changing. I immediately forgot the details experienced during the meditations because I became immersed in my third dimensional world of everyday life. I always knew I could resurrect my notes when the time was right, i.e. now.

By now I had a bevy of spiritual guides working with me when it wasn't so long ago I didn't even know of their existence. How life can change so quickly.

And then on 13th July 1994 I was asked to teach the beginners astrology class at the school during the temporary absence of the teacher. I discovered that I loved to teach, feeling capable, and comfortable, in front of a class.

Crystal Healing

In mid 1994 I began working with crystals, seemingly by 'accident'. In hindsight I realize it was definitely by cosmic design. There was one crystal in particular that became incredibly important to my spiritual growth. This was

'Rootie'. I felt him to be masculine energy. He is a piece of very powerful rutilated quartz and I was introduced to him in a most unusual way.

On my living room coffee table was a large copper bowl filled with gemstones and minerals of all different shapes and sizes. One afternoon when I was walking past this bowl I heard a voice telepathically say "Hi, I'm Rootie".

I turned around and heard the voice again, this time more insistent. "Hi, I'm Rootie". Am I nuts? I thought. Deciding I definitely wasn't I investigated the copper bowl. Where was the voice coming from? I intuitively picked up a smoky quartz crystal with black rutilated needles growing inside, close to its base. Then I heard the voice speak again "Place me on your third eye". My curiosity is always stronger than most other influences so I did as requested.

When I first held this crystal to my forehead, between my eyebrows, I could feel its energy penetrating deep into that area. At first I could only hold it in place for about ten seconds because its current was so strong. But then, over many years of practice, I was able to hold it there for three to five minutes. I visualize the currents as laser beams clearing any energetic dross that blocks my inner vision. This precious crystal helped me to open my third eye chakra to experience incredible multi-dimensional worlds. I worked with Rootie every morning and evening for many years. And still do occasionally, when I feel I need greater inner clarity. He has pride of place beside my bed. I realized then that our spiritual guides come in many forms.

Around this time my telepathic guidance suggested I do an aboriginal style healing on myself, using Rootie and other crystals. I intuitively knew how to do it and will share more about crystal healing later. During the meditation, when I was lying on the floor, arms and legs outstretched with appropriate crystals on and around my body, I was shown how some of my old guides and teachers were preparing to leave so that new ones could take their place. Shadrack was one to leave. Before he left he told me I was an excellent pupil and now ready for a more senior teacher to take his place. I felt very sad to say goodbye and thanked him profusely for his teaching.

I felt completely rejuvenated after the healing experience and practiced it many times.

Crystal Technology

As I'm editing this book for the last time I remember, years ago, being asked by my spiritual guides to research the individual crystals and minerals I have in my collection, and record my findings. I feel connected to these precious natural stones. I used many of these crystals to transform my negative thought patterns and help me gain greater confidence and self-empowerment. The laying-on-of-stones practices came easily to me, as vague soul memories. I understand that crystals are living evolving conscious organisms with an evolutionary role to play. They operate on different frequencies to humans, and vibrate accordingly. Over the past astrological Ages of time many cultures used them as technological and healing tools and I experienced them being used this way in ancient Atlantis, a continent now submerged under the Atlantic ocean. I knew that, when specifically programmed, individual crystals would bring positive change to my mental, emotional, physical and spiritual bodies. I've made a note to write a small book about my findings because there are too many crystals to mention now. I'll itemize how I used four of them.

Phantom quartz: I found that a piece of good quality phantom quartz, when held in the left hand during meditation, helps to access higher states of consciousness and past lives.

Tektite: I wore a piece of this mineral in my bra for many weeks. I experienced emissions of strong rays of powerful energy that moved over my left breast through the meridians and into my heart, pushing through blockages to self-love. When I first started using it I had an impressive bowel purging that released undesirable negativity.

Amethyst: I used this crystal for many purposes. Sometimes I placed it above my crown to help me access higher states of consciousness, and sometimes I placed it on my third eye. I often used it as a wand to purify my energy field.

Lepidolite: This was one of my favourites. I wore it in my bra when I realized it was to be used for acceptance. I needed to accept that my path was different to the norm and that this was O.K. I also needed to accept that I did have ancient wisdom and knowledge inside of me and that the right words would simply come out of my mouth, without thought, when needed.

I taught my students to use specific crystals for healing purposes, asking them to try out different ones on themselves first, before working on others with them. This is because they can affect different people in different ways. My crystals were like a family. I cared for them and they offered me love and healing. I often used to place them outside under a Full Moon and sometimes under a solstice or equinox sun. I would wash them under a cold running tap when they became dusty or cloudy.

During another powerful meditation I was told that I would travel widely and also meet with envy and jealousy. I was asked to keep my own council and speak my truth lovingly. I was also asked to be very discriminating with my daily choices and to weigh and measure everything carefully because impulsiveness would be unwise. (I wish I'd remembered this guidance because impulsiveness hasn't served me and I still occasionally fall into its trap.) My guides assured me of their love and that their guidance was available whenever I needed it.

Sometime later, in my everyday life, I was asked to teach astrology and after much persuasion by many people I finally agreed. How do I do this? I asked myself. The words – "write lessons" - immediately came into my head. I prepared my first lesson and wrote large reminders on flip charts, using brightly coloured pens. My initial three students loved the lesson and wanted more. So I went through the same process each week until I had one year's teaching material prepared. And then there were more students, more writing and more flip charts. Within three years I had four classes a week with up to twelve adult students in each class. I also had many individuals come to me for consultations, astrological readings and guidance. The lessons I wrote became workbooks and they became an astrological trilogy, containing practical exercises, stories and spiritual guidance to help the reader evolve into greater self-understanding and self-knowledge. I felt enormously grateful to be able to serve in this way. These books are available for purchase through my website www.ashtara.com.

The Writing Process

A few days later my inner guidance asked me to begin writing a series of books. They became *Tara, Emissary of Light, Gaia, Our Precious Planet, The Great Cosmic Joke, A Crack in the Cosmic Window* and *A Treasure Trove of Gems*. All I had to do was listen to the inner prompts, which I heard as very clear telepathic transmissions, and to write, with my left hand, whatever I received. Because I had been practicing writing with my non-dominant hand for over a year this was easy. It began when I started working with astrology. At that time I realized I was unable to focus as much as I needed so purchased a book titled *Focus*, but was unable to read it because it was far too intellectual. I needed something more practical so had to find another method. Learning to write with my non-dominant hand was the answer. The purpose of this process was not only to develop greater focus but also to enable heightened intuition.

I practiced and practiced, determined to master the exercise because I didn't want to be controlled by my left-brain, the logical and conditioned brain. I knew this part of the brain is filled with other people's ideas and beliefs and I wanted to discover my own. This dedicated practice worked.

Because I had to focus so intently on keeping the sentences on the page mental interference and static couldn't take over. All I had to do to receive the transmissions was to become quiet and blank my left-brain and wait for the loving voice to speak. The technique I used was that of focused intent. I sometimes imagined pulling down a black blind over my left-brain because I didn't want its chatter to interfere with the transmissions that entered my right brain, the intuitive and abstract part of the brain.

The teachings I received are very potent and their messages are even more vital for humanity today than they were then. The transmissions became five books. Each book contains important messages about humanity's future, and the information deeply resonated with my heart and soul. When I was about half way through writing *Gaia, Our Precious Planet* I began crying streams of heart-breaking tears. The message was very clear. Human psychic baggage contaminates and pollutes the Earth's energy field. Unless humanity changes, internally and externally, there will be many more global earth problems. They were outlined graphically and I felt that every word rang true. Change must happen, it is part of humanity's evolutionary process. If individuals are unwilling to consciously change by doing their inner psychological housekeeping then external change will be forced upon them. Since then I've done my best to prepare and teach my many students and clients how to identify and transform their dense psychological patterns through self-awareness and the light of higher consciousness.

The message downloads increased in volume and continued for many years. I wrote down most of them and all were valuable. In one I was asked to teach the importance of personal responsibility; meaning that each of us needs to accept, and take responsibility for, everything we create in our lives. We do this creation process through our emotions and thoughts, usually unconsciously. I have taught this truth, zealously.

During my daily meditation practice a gentle and compassionate spiritual guide called Mary became a regular visitor giving me much valuable advice. At this time I still wasn't sure whether she was Mother Mary or Mary Magdalen. She said I would be teaching about light frequencies, which didn't mean very much to me at the time. She also guided me to the books I needed to read plus healing techniques to learn, some using crystals.

Introduction to Sai Baba

Sometimes during my regular meditation practices I experienced past life flashes that helped explain what was happening in my current life. I was able to extract the essence of the particular psychological issue, and apply my understanding of the healing action needed to bring about inner balance, with positive results. I did not become emotionally involved in the particular story.

During meditation one morning in August 1994 my eagle guide asked me to jump upon his back so he could fly me to where we needed to go. I did so, totally trusting the experience. It felt exhilarating. We landed beside a calm and clear lake and there I saw an unusual human-like figure. Creating in my mind an image of a clear blue lake was one of the techniques I used to access a relaxed mental state. However this was the first time my eagle guide flew me to this place. I didn't question the experience rather I was curious as to where I was being taken. The individual I saw was wearing an orange robe. He was small and slight with a mass of black frizzy hair. His face was unusual – a mixture between an Australian Aboriginal and a Fijian. He grinned cheekily, saying, as he handed me a strange powdered substance, that he was Sai Baba. He said he was giving me the ash, called vibhuti, to use regularly because we both carried the same vibration and therefore we were equals. He also said we had worked together in a previous life. I felt the truth of these words resonate in my heart but didn't have any conscious memory of that life.

This celestial meeting motivated me to find out more about this living Indian holy man. During the next few months, whenever I visited a bookstore, a book written about him would magically drop from a shelf or I would be instantly attracted to one. So again I learned about my spiritual guides after they made themselves known. The vibhuti, or ash, contains Sai Baba's electronic vibratory patterning and he consciously manifests it into his hands.

When he visited me in another dimension he was alive on the 3D plane. His home and ashram is in India and tens of thousands of people from all around the world visited him every day. He built many schools and an amazing hospital outside Bangalore. He was nearly ninety years old when he passed away - only a few years ago. I had the privilege of being invited by him to visit his home/ashram some years later. I did so – and that is another story.

White Buffalo Woman

On 8th September 1994, during a deep meditation, I was introduced to White Buffalo woman, the spirit of a particular grouping of stars. She suggested I begin making essences from flowers as an earth based healing project in order to balance my spiritual experiences and philosophical studies. So I did. I studied the healing properties of Australian bush flower essences with Ian White, a world authority, and was soon making my own from my garden. I loved working with the beautiful flowers of nature.

Often, during my meditations, I would be taken to a healing temple in what appeared to be a crystal City of Light. All the buildings seemed to be made from a clear crystalline material. Some were shaped like clusters of earth crystals. The space inside the temple was high, light and uncluttered. As soon as I entered I felt a blissful peace descend upon me. I felt healing and energizing currents move through my entire body as if I was receiving an infusion of pure love juice.

This was apparently needed because, whenever I became overwhelmed with deep emotions that left me ineffectual and weak, I was unable to meditate. My marriage was declining and I was allowing fear and a sense of powerlessness to rule my state of mind. Both my husband and I were suffering. I felt unable to communicate to him in a way he would understand and I was also afraid to say "no" to his aggressive demands. I was aware our life-paths were diverging however I was determined to work on myself to ensure the best outcome. I didn't want our marriage to fail, as had that of my parents. When I was in a weakened emotional state I wasn't able to receive the spiritual training apparently necessary for my evolutionary progress. So I was given energy healing to balance my disharmonious state of being.

During my meditations throughout this year Sai Baba visited me many times and we became good friends. He made me laugh. I perceived him as a cosmic joker and I really enjoyed his visits and good humour. His training, he advised, was to help me to understand, experience and become, love.

During other meditations he gave me spiritual global service tasks. One was to send love and light energy, the highest frequency possible to attain on Earth, to the tectonic plates of the globe, in order to 'oil' them. I was often asked to focus on sending these high frequencies to the 'Ring of Fire' tectonic plates in the South Pacific. Another task given was to send the same frequencies into the hearts and minds of specific world leaders who were preparing to make important global decisions. I did these practices reverently. I felt honoured to serve the planet, and humanity, in this way and never questioned my guidance because it felt right.

On one occasion I was taken to view a group of world leaders who were seated around a large boardroom table. They were meeting in a country unfamiliar to me. I wasn't able to identify the country however I felt it was in Europe or maybe Russia. I generated as much love and light into my heart and mind as I could and then focused my thoughts on their children and grandchildren. I intuitively felt that, by becoming attentive to the love they have for their children and grandchildren, the leaders would make the best decisions, from their heart; ones that were for the greater good of generations to come.

On another occasion I was shown the future where I was telepathically communicating to a central city. I appeared to be living in two places, one on the city's outskirts, and the other on a space station. I noticed my communiqués formed grid-like patterns of light. Children were learning telepathy at school and I felt this to be an important progression from our current way of educating them. Some of the schools were built into the earth with roofs made of a glass-like substance. The Earth's energy was important, and needed, in order to facilitate learning and keep the students grounded and 'earthed'. It was around this time I realized we humans are like radio sets. We receive energy transmissions into our minds, from different channels and frequencies, and then transmit them, according to our level of consciousness. If we are non-loving we transmit this energy, passing it on to others. Our precious planet receives and experiences our output, according to the quality of energy we transmit. Currently our collective transmissions are mostly disharmonious. I pray this book will help to correct this situation.

Introduction to the Sacred Circle Dance, Paneurythmy

During October 1994, in my everyday material life, I was on the alert for something new to come into my life because this was indicated in my birth chart. By this time I was able to follow the transiting (travelling) planetary energies daily, via the astrological Ephemeris. This is like a logbook of planetary movements for each day of any year. On this day I expected Mercury, the archetypal messenger of the gods, to deliver a new message to me. I didn't know how this would manifest and was curious to find out.

On the anticipated day I found an esoteric science magazine in my mailbox posted to me from a group I hadn't heard of before. I read the literature carefully but nothing connected to my heart. And then, near the bottom of the last page, I saw a small advertisement for a workshop on Paneurythmy, a Bulgarian sacred circle dance. I felt my soul leap with joy and my heart expand as I read the promotional material and decided to act upon the uplifting feeling.

I travelled to Adelaide to participate in, and learn as best I could, this ancient sacred dance. Within a few minutes of beginning the dance practice I experienced a past life remembrance. I had the vision, and experienced the sensations, of dancing in what seemed to be a temple in pre-historic Greece. I saw myself in white robes loosely tied at the waist by a gold rope. I loved this heart-opening dance and felt I had returned home to it.

I realized then that my formerly dark inner cave was becoming light filled through the joy I was creating in my life. The teacher told the group that this dance had been taught and practiced by the Essene community, a group of adherents to the gnostic teachings, during the time of Jesus. I intuitively knew I had once been an Essene so this information came as no surprise. The gnostic teachings emphasize the need for individuals to walk their own spiritual path to find truth within.

At this time I was refining my astrological understanding by training myself to feel the planetary movements in my mind and body to ascertain truth. I was beginning to identify, through feeling, urges and motivation, each of their different energetic characteristics.

Through my experiences I learned that we each have the universe within and that the ancient hermetic wisdom "As Above – so below" is true.

A Scientific Experiment

During this year I was also trained to experience and record scientific material. This was not our normal science.

The first experiment I was shown, on one of my starry adventures, was that of a spiral, spinning like a top and accelerating at an incredible speed until it emitted a tone, a sound. This, I was told, was how the universe was formed. Our bodies are similar. Our chakras, spinning centres of energy situated in our etheric body, act as spirals and, as they become clear of accumulated life times of psychological debris, begin to spin more evenly. Then the spin accelerates and so does our vibratory rate. When our spin increases to a particular level we begin to emit a sound that evolved spirit beings from higher vibratory levels pick up and can respond to. Apparently all energy works this way. The more inwardly clean and pure we humans are then the more we begin to vibrate at a higher speed, much like a tuning fork. Then, when the tone is pure, we spiral into higher dimensions. It is then lighter beings can connect with us.

The Council of Nine

On December 14th 1994, during a deep meditation, I experienced my first contact with the Council of Nine from the star system of Sirius. They introduced themselves as a group consciousness and said we would be working together for some time. They also said that when I chanted the Sanskrit mantra Om Na Mah Shi Va Ya I would be able to access my akashic records. I understand these are soul records stored in the akasha, the subtle etheric field that surrounds the body. I'm not sure whether I did this at the time but I did buy a C.D. of the chant when I travelled to Nepal some years later and practiced it then. I often accessed my akashic records to gain clearer understanding of my soul's journey.

And then, two weeks later on 28th December, I was advised that:

"Today is a day of extreme importance on a planetary level. It is the beginning of a New Age. Be aware and watch."

I forgot this information until I came to revise my

journal notes in 2011. Many people have asked me when is, or was, the beginning of The Age of Aquarius. I'd thought it was 21st December 2012 –however it seems as though it was 28th December 1994.

During this year I grew to appreciate and highly value the beauty and bounty of Mother Earth and the sustenance she provides to every living creature upon her. I learned to open my heart chakra, one of the energy centres in our etheric body, to feel and radiate the vibration of love. The love I was developing was a spiritualized love, a deep soul love of God, whose essence is within every living thing. It is beyond human love.

The energetic infusion of self-generated love developed deeper self-understanding and appreciation of other's paths. I gradually realized the energetic connections we have to one another and our universe. It's as if we are all individual cells within the spiritual 'body' of our Supreme Creator.

One of the tools I used to progress my spiritual growth was to practise toning sacred sounds until I felt the vibration physically connect my heart and soul. As resonance developed I sometimes felt my lungs 'stretching' as if to accommodate a larger heart. This was often painful but I persisted. I realized that each sound and word vibrates at different frequencies of light so I decided to tone the names of other sacred deities. This dedicated spiritual process generated greater light and love within me, and ease of connection to higher dimensional realities. Self-generated love, sound and spiritual light became my healing tools.

A higher level of intelligence began to emerge as I learned to differentiate between intellect and intelligence. Intellect develops through the left hemisphere of the brain and is limited to logic and rational thought. Intelligence is holistic and grows through a combination of instinct and intuition when mind, body and heart-felt feelings align. My passionate intention was to build within myself, in a stable Taurus manner, a strong psychological love-based foundation from which to progress spiritually. I understood that a slow step-by-step growth process would enable the development of wisdom.

PART 2

DEDICATION TO THE LIGHT

1995 - The Sacred Journey

During meditation on January 4th 1995 I was told by the Council of Nine that I would be doing soul readings for clients combining astrology and numerology, and that I needed to keep on learning more about both subjects. I did as they asked and, since then, have worked with thousands of clients. Also during this meditation my guides asked that I become aware when they downloaded extra light frequencies into my crown chakra because I could turn the pressure up or down. I developed sensitivity to these 'light' downloads and learned to manage them. I was also asked to listen very carefully to the messages given because soon I would be speaking them. Words would just come out of my mouth naturally and intuitively. They said I was a scribe, passing on information, and this was one way I would heal others. I was also asked to write everything down as it was given to me.

The following day the Council told me that I am originally from Sirius B, a gateway to the Orion constellation, and this is where my healing 'light city' is located. I was also asked to distribute my love essence around the world through deeds, and the use of my creative imagination. They then said that "Focus is most important", and "prepare your self for devotional work every day".

Then I was taken to Africa and shown the tectonic plates where horrific devastation is to occur. I would see it and be safe, however I was to tell others, prepare myself spiritually and trust the process. Focus and connecting to the higher realms were the keys that would enable me to trust. They asked that I operate my life in present time, and, just in case life became too serious, to laugh and have fun.

The advice contained in the latter sentence hasn't always been the easiest to do even though Sai Baba did his best. I've been a serious and introverted person – however I love to dance. I'm still working on creating more fun through free creative dance.

In early January I received a message from the Archangel Michael who asked me to always be aware of my body. He said that I enter meditation very easily however I need to learn that whatever I negatively think about will create an instant pain in my body to warn me that the thought was inappropriate. Archangel Michael also said that my guides are always present, in my body. And I must observe very carefully my thoughts and corresponding body sensations at the time of the pain because my body acts as a tool for deciphering truth. He asked me to become aware of Nature's messages and signs and used as an example the birds. He said they are here to bring people joy and assist the opening of hearts to Nature's love.

Since receiving this message I have experienced an incredible amount of joy from Mother Nature, especially the early morning birdsong. Where I live in Australia the birds are prolific and I love being woken up by the laughing of kookaburras, even if it is very early in the morning.

The next few days were spent without communion because I became emotionally upset. The upsets were always connected to my husband. My marriage was still declining and I was doing the best I could to heal myself from negative attitudes. I loved my husband and wanted the marriage to work but there were problems. I still felt powerless, ineffectual and weak. Astrology, and the self-knowledge I developed through it, helped me so much. I was confident about my alternate life in other dimensions, and with my work, but I wasn't confident about confronting a critical and overbearing masculine force. Obviously I still had inner work to do.

A few days later I began to receive transmissions for another book, A Crack in the Cosmic Window, a series of heart-opening messages connected to the theme of love.

Around this time I began to write astrology articles and some spiritual magazines asked for regular contributions. I enjoyed sharing what I had learned. I also became aware that words flowed very easily when operating in "now" time. When I'm not operating in present time, words are difficult to formulate and put into succinct sentences.

Some days later my guides advised that most things would soon change in my life. They said that the more I became filled with love energy (I call it love juice) the more I'd be able to see clearly and act decisively on my own behalf. My "task", or "mission" to be given is totally dependant upon my level of commitment to my spiritual practices, deep breathing, yoga and regular daily walking.

I enjoy yoga and became interested in it in 1958

when I was preparing to give birth to my first child, in Fiji. Doctors were few and far between, especially in the remote mining area where we lived. However I wasn't in the slightest bit worried. It was a regular occurrence to see the native women give birth to their babies in the fields so I figured that if they could do it so could I. But I felt I needed a tool to help me understand, and prepare my mind and body for the birthing process.

On a holiday to Australia I purchased a DIY yoga book specifically geared to child birthing. I practiced the yoga exercises everyday, in order to stretch my pelvis and learn to breathe properly. I found I was a natural at the postures, as if I'd learnt this ancient philosophical science in another time and place. I gave birth to two babies in this country, very easily and naturally with no problems whatsoever. The doctor came to catch the firstborn – a boy, and the nurse looked after me in the small four-bed hospital. She was the only worker there. I had a lovely holiday, as the only patient, learning how to care for and nurture my baby boy. A doctor didn't make the second birth but it didn't matter. I was at a different hospital this time, a larger one.

Amazingly the attendant nursing sister had been trained at the same hospital in Australia, and at the same time, as when I had worked there before I married. I had worked in the administration section. We didn't meet at that time but had a chat as she delivered my baby girl. We had a very warm connection. She told me that she wished her fellow countrywoman were as capable and calm as I was. The next day I played nursemaid to the young Indian mothers in the hospital, enjoying the experience. However, their lack of understanding about the correct purpose of the toilet and bath created a few cleanliness problems but I soon had it sorted.

Gaia's Ascension

Towards the end of January 1995 I received a gentle reminder from my guides to become more observant and aware of nature's sounds. I was also asked to become more discerning in interactive human situations by tuning in to the truth of my feelings.

A few days later, during meditation, my guides told me that Gaia, Mother Earth, a living, breathing organism, was in the process of ascending to a higher frequency of light because it was part of her evolutionary process. They said that the 'birthing' would soon take place. Humans were being prepared to transition with Gaia, from the density of 3D matter into a frequency band of greater light because it is part of our evolutionary process. They told me it was important to continue writing my thoughts, insights and messages because, in time, I would co-exist in other worlds.

Sometime during the month of February I chose to look into my future. I had done so much past life work to clear myself of globules of gunk from ancient memories that I wanted a lift, a fun activity. So, during a relaxed meditative state I programmed my mind to take me into the future. I felt my eyelids fluttering at an incredible rate of speed, like the wings of bees hovering over a plant. I took myself into the future easily and was shown two scenarios.

One was so shocking it greatly upset me. I was shown again some of the devastation to come, especially to Africa, and it was too much for my heart and soul to bear. My body reacted with shock and nausea. The other scene was much easier to accept. I was on stage sharing my cosmic experiences with large groups of people. Both scenarios involved me instigating two totally different group-healing processes, using my voice to tone special soul resonating sounds.

I decided that I didn't want to play this future game ever again and that I'd much rather keep my mind in present time.

A few days later I received word that I had passed all the other astrology exams necessary at this point in time. Hurrah! This was a cause for celebration. There were four exams associated with this first level of study. One was based on astronomy and chart calculation techniques. This was the exam where I had to be supported out of the examination room. I received a high distinction for this subject. The others were based on astrological psychology. As mentioned earlier I had found the technical examination process incredibly stressful because of subconscious fears relating to making a mistake. I had chosen to leave school when I was fifteen so I could work to financially support my mother, who was bringing up three children on her own. I had little academic training.

At the time of the astrology exams I believed I didn't know enough due to insufficient education. The main thing was, I passed and felt a great sense of accomplishment for a job well done. Now I was well on the way to becoming a professional astrologer.

Around this time a new light entered my life in the form of a lovable little fluffy dog I adopted from the animal welfare league. He chose me. He began barking when I walked past his kennel but he was in the area of dogs waiting to be collected by new owners so I didn't take any notice of him. After inspecting the available dogs and not finding a connecting spark, he barked again so I stopped to pat him. I felt an instant soul connection. He wanted me and I wanted to adopt him but he wasn't available. I spoke to the staff and told them of my interest and left my phone number. They told me to look for another dog.

I did but couldn't connect to another one. Two weeks later I received a call to collect him - if I still wanted him. Of course I did. I loved him with all my heart. I felt him to be a very wise old soul, full of compassion and love. He seemed familiar as if I'd known him before. And this was apparently the case.

Close to my seventh birthday my father rescued a lost and very bedraggled small dog from the side of the road where he had been dumped. It was the best birthday present I had ever received. I loved him so much however he was only with me three months before he was accidently run over by a car. He died and I wasn't allowed to have another one. My spiritual guides told me that my new dog was an incarnation of that one and would be with me for a very long time. And he was. He passed in 2009 when he was seventeen years old.

A few days later my guides asked me to reflect on how far I'd come during the past year. They said I was still to practice listening to my inner voice because, soon, I would be naturally speaking from it.

They continued, saying that I was also learning to re-ignite my intuitive brain to its fullest capacity, as I apparently used to do in a former life in Atlantis. One of my major weaknesses has been learning to identify, formulate and then express verbally, and in written word, what I know and feel to be true. I was also told that my mind has the ability to understand vast concepts however it has been difficult to find the right words to convey my understanding. Therefore I was to continue listening to my inner voice so I could learn to trust that the words would come when needed.

I feel the word 'Atlantis' needs some explanation. During my many adventures into past lives I experienced living situations in both Atlantis, an ancient civilization on a now submerged continent in the Atlantic Ocean and the even more ancient country, Lemuria, or Mu, formerly situated in the Pacific Ocean. My soul memories of living in these two civilizations were very real so I know they existed.

Many years later, when I spent a great deal of time in the Andean mountains of Peru and Bolivia, I experienced other memories of those ancient times, and gained an incredible amount of valuable information. I am an old soul, like many people on Earth, and my soul memories are close to the surface of my consciousness. Specific places, people and situations activate them.

A few days later I received another valuable message instructing me to teach the human spiritual evolutionary process. Human evolution accelerates when an individual consciousness awakens to experience broader self-understanding. We are all connected by a fine web of light particles (light being information) and, when the 'awakening to truth' message is received through one mind it automatically sends the message through the etheric web to all who are tuned in to the same wave band. This enables us to expand our essential nature, open our minds to endless possibilities and understand there is always time to grow spiritually. At some point critical mass occurs. A new and lighter thought form (software) takes shape within the hard drive of humanity's collective mind. As individuals expand their conscious understanding of themselves so the Universe, a living, evolving organism, expands as well.

This internal consciousness raising process has its external manifestation in the Internet, the world-wide-web.

Colour Therapy

During 1995 I received from my guides a great deal of spiritual healing. They also showed me many techniques to help me heal myself. One particular technique involved visualizing a white vortex of energy, acting much like a tornado, cleaning out from my heart chakra all that was not love. When I completed this process I was asked to fill my heart with a vibrant colour green, similar to the colour of green apples. Then I was asked to visualize a golden light all around my body. The next part was to imagine and feel different colours entering my chakras, the spinning wheels of energy situated in the etheric field of the human body. Then I was asked to use the colour violet, and then silver, around my body and finally to place a silver pyramid over my entire body, to seal the self-generated loving energy. I was asked to repeat this healing modality many times, whenever I felt out of love.

Colours carry frequencies. The more clear and vibrant the colour the more valuable it is as a therapy. Colour therapy is a wonderful tool to help holistically re-balance the mental, emotional, spiritual and physical bodies.

I was being trained in many healing modalities, all of which I practiced regularly and then, as the years went by, forgot to do so. Until now! However, since that time I have always chosen to wear light, clear, bright colours. I wasn't able to wear bright red until 2007, and that is a later story.

Another message I received this year was about the Earth's crust and how it is vibrational. It becomes dense from too much toxicity, often as a result of inconsiderate and inhumane human behaviour as well as human negative thought patterns, especially those of greed, corruption and power. These accumulative dark thought patterns form a dense energetic 'fog' that permeates and contaminates the earth's crust. The following transmission from Sai Baba is self-explanatory.

"The earth is scattered with minerals and crystals that help to balance this toxicity. However, when these are taken away deliberately, that balance is broken. This is the state of our planet now. It cannot go on in this condition forever. Human love vibrations, sent by groupings of caring people, help to address this imbalance. However, it may not be enough to maintain equilibrium".

The Wonderful Properties of Zeolite

Sometime during this year I was introduced to the mineral zeolite. My husband began working with it physically and I chose to work with it metaphysically. He was working with an exploration mining company at the time and zeolite was the mineral under investigation.

Through my meditation enquiries I was given information about how it could be used as a healing tool to cure many maladies. When ground into a fine powder and mixed with water or juice it could be taken internally. Apparently it is used this way in Cuba, Russia and other places around the world, but not in Australia. Because its structure is porous it can be used as a 'clean-up' agent to attract and contain human negativity. I spoke to my husband about my metaphysical research and the results obtained from the case studies.

Zeolite is also used to clean up and store uranium radiation, as was the case in the Chernobyl disaster. I did my best to inform and share the information, and the powder, with my students. Many of them experimented with it to heal themselves from all sorts of illnesses and diseases, including cancer. It certainly did the job I was informed it would do.

On 2nd March 1995 I said farewell to the group of light beings assigned to teach me trust, wisdom, integrity and the other qualities. I had apparently embodied their training and was ready to move on to another vibratory level with a different group of teachers and guides. Before they left they said I was in the process of mounting the 'cardinal cross'. According to esoteric astrology this is the third and highest level of the human soul's evolutionary developmental process. As we become conscious of our dense psychological patterning and choose to rise above it then tests to this commitment take place. The first 'cross' in the evolutionary development process is the mutable cross where we learn life lessons related to the mutable zodiacal signs, those of Gemini/Virgo/Sagittarius and Pisces. This process can take many life times.

The next cross to mount is the fixed cross and the soul challenges come through the fixed signs of the zodiac as Taurus/Scorpio/Leo and Aquarius. The psychological issues associated with these signs are often the most difficult to overcome because of their 'fixed' and stubborn nature. Overcoming them can take many more lifetimes. The cardinal cross is the third of the series of crosses and the signs involved are Aries/Libra/Cancer and Capricorn. Many humans are currently, and consciously, accelerating their soul's evolutionary development in sync with Gaia's spiritual evolutionary development. This evolutionary developmental process is described in more detail in my book *Esoteric Astrology, The Astrology of the Soul.*

One of my main lessons still to master was that of

developing the confidence (Aries) to assert my personal needs, with integrity and love. My guides recommended I take specific flower essences to assist the process. I was also asked to become aware of how, why and when I allow nervous tension to take over my body. It was by paying close attention to this timing that I could access the cause of my disharmony and imbalance. They also suggested I play and relax more because this would bring my emotions into balance, so I created once a month 'Play Days' for my students. We had such fun playing ball games, swimming in my pool, and playing with our special toys.

The Obelisk

Something unusual and unexpected happened during meditation on the 4th March. One of the processes I used to go into meditation was to imagine myself walking slowly up a series of twelve steps within my body, from my heart to crown, and then wait, at a place about half a metre above my crown. I imagine this place as a platform or station. Prior to the 'steps' process I spent time generating the frequency of love within my heart. This was my standard feeling practice. I had trained myself to completely blank my left-brain chatter and relax my body, and I seemed to do this process easily. Then I would wait patiently, often for 5-10 minutes, and sometimes even longer. It was a peaceful and loving space and I could have stayed there a long time. I had a non-expectant attitude. Occasionally nothing occurred

On this day, after a reasonable waiting period, I was greeted by a small group of little egg-shaped light green, almost see-through, beings that felt incredibly supportive and loving. They invited me to go on board their space ship. In complete trust I accepted and we travelled at incredible speeds, apparently landing in a different galaxy to that of our Milky Way. There I was shown a huge black column that I likened to an obelisk. It had hieroglyphics carved all over it. I was asked to remember it because it was an intergalactic symbol for love and peace. I did not record any other details nor did I reflect upon the experience afterwards. It had seemed so natural, right and familiar that I didn't question. I felt so connected to the little beings and knew they came to me in love, harmony and peace. I realized it was the love frequency I'd developed within me that enabled them to interact with me.

The Archangel Michael

During the early part of this year I began receiving transmissions from the Archangel Michael as well as other light beings, so my inner life was busy. As mentioned previously I was also involved in planetary service work, and this practice continued on a regular basis.

In my 3D life I was teaching myself to dance the sacred circle dance, Paneurythmy. I felt so connected to it. As I danced I felt my vibration rise to a higher level as love and joy filled my heart. My astrological studies continued and I applied all I learnt to myself, choosing to be a 'guinea pig' for interior research. I wasn't willing to share what I learnt unless it could be applied practically to life, and achieve excellent results.

My life was very fulfilling and joyous. The only dark spot was my relationship with my husband. I shared my experiences with him even though I knew I could receive derision and criticism. He found it difficult to understand why so many people wanted to learn from me.

And then, on 6th March during a meditation practice, I was introduced to a very tall illumined being with enormous wings. I saw him clearly and he felt very loving and gentle. This was the Archangel Michael or how he chose to show himself to me. Or maybe how I perceived him. He told me he was replacing some of my teachers and that he preferred me to refer to him as Michael. He said that both he and Sai Baba would instruct and train me, in their different ways. He also said that I had earned the respect of the Spiritual Hierarchy and that I too was a 'Tall One' before my descent into matter. He said I am to once again return to this status.

Dedication to the Light

During meditation, on the morning of 21st March 1995, the day of the Aries Equinox, I dedicated myself to God's work. "Thy Will be done, not mine, be done and I will serve the Spiritual Hierarchy to the best of my ability." Following this sincere and heart-felt dedication I observed a huge beam of brilliant white light descend over me and then noticed a door open in front of me. Clouds of billowing smoke poured forth and out came a very large groggy demon. I asked St. Germaine, another of my guides, to take it to the light, and he did. I learned the next day, from Michael, that this demon was my ego.

Michael asked me to continue focusing on love, light and compassion as I had been instructed to do for years, and to override self-doubt and other negative thoughts with those of love.

Two days later, during a meditation, I saw myself becoming immersed in brilliant white light. I was asked to open the door I noticed in front of me and, when I did, saw a huge precipice. I was asked to jump off this precipice into the abyss, without fear. I did, and felt as if I was a leaf gently falling towards the earth. I completely trusted the process and landed at the Tall One's feet. We embraced and he congratulated me on overcoming my fear, and in learning to trust.

I understand now that some of the mystical practices I was given were to enable their manifestation in the 3D plane. First they needed to take place in the etheric. It's a similar process to how our thoughts and emotions create our every-day reality. Most people are unconscious of this process. Our spiritual evolutionary destiny is to evolve into super- consciousness, or Christ conscious, humans. In order to do so we must train ourselves to become observers of the way in which we create our lives. The observer process enables the light of higher consciousness to infuse our cells following many 'Ah-Ha' self-realization moments. When our bodies carry greater spiritual light we no longer react to emotionally charged situations, are healthier, and live longer and happier lives.

The next day I had a short visitation from a group of three light beings called The Elohim however I found their energy far too high a frequency for me handle. I couldn't maintain focus and clarity so was unable to work with them.

In the everyday 3D world I conducted my first Paneurythmy dance class in my beautiful garden. Many of my friends had previously asked me to share the dance and I did so gladly. I loved this heart-opening joyful dance. At the conclusion my little dog joined us in the centre of the circle to absorb the high frequency love energy created by the group through the dance.

During my morning meditation the following day I was asked to send light and love to Uluru, the great sacred rock in the heart of Australia, to the Rainbow Serpent and the ancient land of Australia. I performed this task willingly and happily, without questioning.

And then, on 4th April, during another meditation, I was taken to a mountaintop and introduced to Peter Deunov, who said he was to be my inner dancing teacher. He was a physical 20th century Bulgarian Spiritual Master who gave Paneurythmy to the world. He adopted his spiritual name, Beinso Douno, and passed on in 1944. He taught the dance for many years of his life, in the Rila Mountains of Bulgaria, and referred to it as the New Yoga for the Age of Light. He asked me to study his writings and teachings because he had chosen me as his pupil. He went on to say that there is a science and philosophy behind his teaching that convey his understanding of life and the cosmos. I learned later that he is an Ascended Spiritual Master of a similar vibration to Sai Baba.

It was some days following this experience that I decided to stop attending astrology classes because I felt the same material was being recycled. I had not missed a class for two and a half years, often attending two and three times a week. I felt I had learned as much as I could from my wonderful teacher and needed to explore broader horizons.

My Understanding of Creation

I understand that creation consists of infinite dimensions of life vibrating at different speeds. Most of us think we operate on only one frequency range, the third dimensional (3D) one. However, consider all the different frequency ranges needed to operate our radio and TV. To change TV channels, or radio stations, we can press a remote control, or turn a dial. We humans share these frequency spaces. We can't see these frequencies but they are there. We can learn to feel them in our bodies and 'tune-up' to the higher ones. This is what I was trained to do.

I learned that we live and operate on a third dimensional (3D) frequency band. Psychological baggage keeps our frequency range at this low vibratory rate. The more dense and heavy is the baggage the lower the personal vibratory level. This dense baggage contains dark emotions such as fear, hate, revenge, jealousy, envy, arrogance, greed, control etc. The greater the degree of baggage the slower our life-force energy vibrates. Animals pick up our vibratory levels and react accordingly. Insects only bite when we emit anger or fear.

Energy cannot be destroyed, however it can be transmuted, or alchemized, into a different state. This process applies also to psychological energy. Emotions and thoughts are energy in motion and emotional energy is created through thought. Thoughts are based on perceptions and experience. Many of our thoughts come from childhood conditioning and some can be soul experiences from other lives that are buried deep in our subconscious realms.

If a mind is unconscious and unaware of this realm then the dense buried emotions containing the dark memories naturally attracts like energies. Energetic mass accumulates and, over time, illness develops in the cellular area of the body containing the dense mass. The illness can become life threatening. Some open-minded doctors and scientists are beginning to realize, and accept, this esoteric truth.

I chose to transform and purify my inner world as if

my life depended upon it. And perhaps it did. When I began cleaning up my psyche I was able to raise my frequency levels to consciously generate finer light. I chose to constantly think and act upon illuminating, compassionate, generous, appreciative and loving thoughts and often the instant manifestation of these thoughts took place. Through this process I was able to experience ethereal and non-physical life forms. This spiritual path requires devotion to the transmutation of dense vibrational matter, our psychological density (baggage).

When we pass on we leave, not only our physical bodies, but also the 3D frequency realm. We continue our journey elsewhere, as a spirit and soul. The dimensional level we experience is dependant upon the electronic vibratory patterning of our soul at the time of transition. Our consciousness is eternal and we are all connected, as one.

However, we do not have to die to experience Oneness and the state of absolute bliss, as you will read further on in the book. We also do not need to die to experience other dimensional realms. I was trained to become an inter-dimensional hopper and to interact with light beings in higher and finer realms of experience. Others may also have been trained as I was and if so, I'd like to hear from them. This journey has been incredibly enlightening as well as transformational.

An Important Lesson

A week or so later I suffered a most violent psychic attack. This was a result of not honouring myself as much as I honoured another, a supposed friend. She taught me much, about her envy, jealousy and revenge and how these emotions are so poisonous to someone who doesn't harbour them. I had to go to bed for five days, nauseous and comatose, not able to think or move. When I eventually 'came to' I told her to leave. She congratulated me, saying that I had learned a lot about dark energy during her stay. In other words she knew what she was doing when she projected her negative thoughts onto me. She did it deliberately, with the aim of weakening me.

I learned that I needed to be more discriminating with those I allow into my space. I had given myself totally to this 'friend' who had come to me ill and weak. I nurtured and cared for her back to health. However when I went out one night with my husband to watch our granddaughter perform in a children's ballet, having been unable to purchase a ticket for the friend, the attack began. As soon as I sat in my theatre seat the waves of nausea overtook me. I couldn't see anything on the stage, became weak unable to move or think, and had to be carried out of the theatre, taken home and put to bed.

This jealous and envious person also borrowed one of my favourite books before I told her to leave. I asked her to post it to me when she finished reading it. A few weeks later it returned and, when I opened the package a heavy and sickening energy burst out from the book, much like dark smoke, and I had to quickly throw it in the garbage bin before it infected me.

I then remembered that something similar had happened when I first attended astrology school. I had wanted to buy my first set of tarot cards and the deck recommended was the well known Aleister Crowley one. So I purchased it. When I took it home and opened the sealed package a horrible dark energy 'flew' out and I felt sick. I immediately re-sealed the package. I knew it wasn't for me. The next time I went to class I told the teacher about my experience and she assured me that others had not felt the same. I realized then how super sensitive I was to negative human psychological energy currents and that, if I ever went into negativity myself, I would attract like to me – so I could learn the importance of staying positive.

I was also learning to be far more discriminating with what, and who, I allowed into my space.

During meditation the next day I was taken for a healing to Sirius B and it was an interesting process. Sirius is another star system within the constellation of Cancer, and my birth chart Sun is in this sign, and conjunct Sirius. At the beginning of the healing process I was carefully strapped vertically against a clear 'glass' wall, legs and arms outstretched. The clear material of the wall appeared to contain healing vibrations. The group who met me were the Council of Nine from Sirius and they bombarded me with the high frequency of love and light. They emphasized that my lesson was to continue giving out love while honouring myself, and, when the other person does not honour me, to move away from them. I can still love them, but detach emotionally from them. I was advised that further ascension could occur and growth speeded up when this self-honouring was integrated.

I later realized that my experiences with human energy were a training ground for me to understand the universal energy system. When individual or collective psychological energy is dense and of a low vibratory level it affects all within its sphere of influence. I also learnt that all living organisms have an energy field and that the collective level of human consciousness is energetically connected to earth changes. When many people spew forth negative energy then Mother Earth, a living organism, experiences it in her energy field and cleanses accordingly. Earthquakes and volcanoes are the physical manifestations of her release. I'm sure innovative and open-minded scientists will discover this esoteric truth, and maybe some have already done so.

Towards the end of this month I was spiralled to the 32nd dimension to greet the Elohim, Creator Gods, acting on behalf of The One. They introduced themselves to me as Andromeda, Alpha and Theta. It was a very brief meeting because I still needed finer tuning before I could interact with them at their high frequency of light. It was the highest dimension I had experienced. As I understand it dimensions cannot be measured by 3D linear thinking however they can be experienced as different frequencies of light operating on specific wave bands.

A Cosmic Identity

During my meditation the following day I was taken to the Elohim again. They told me their task was to teach me about energy and vibration. They said I would be given information on the correct use of energy and how it can heal karma and past life debris and, as I learn and experience, I am to record my findings. I was asked to pass on this information because it is necessary for human evolution. The group said they would alternate their teaching with those of Sai Baba.

On the following Sunday I visited the nearby Sai Baba centre and enjoyed the experience. I felt at home and comfortable during the service. However I was concerned about how men and women had to separate and sit on different sides of the room, even though I understood it was for energetic purposes to enable more concentrated devotion. The next day, during meditation, I was told that I would meet Sai Baba physically, as well as spending more time with him in the etheric planes.

Early in May and during meditation I was taken to the high dimension again, where the tall beings reside, and saw an incredible kaleidoscope of brilliant colours. These tall energies are my soul group, I was told, and they want me to spiritually grow to their height. They emanated a silver/gold colour. They circled me, toning pure notes, sounding a little like a gentle soothing breeze. I felt their waves of love engulf and fill me and it was a wonderfully nourishing sensation. Their vibration was exceedingly fine yet I could feel a light pressure on my crown chakra. They merged into me and it felt blissful, ecstatic and so right.

Then my eagle transport took me down the dimensional levels to above India - to greet Sai Baba. He appeared in his unique semi- human form and blessed me with his sacred ash. Then he moved his hands down my aura in a staccato type motion, from the top of my head to heart level. Always downwards! He was moving energy in my field and I felt it. We then faced each other and he said I needed to reinforce my commitment to my spiritual work and to develop greater courage. I also needed to develop a state of emotional and mental balance before I acted. Therefore I was to focus on attaining this harmonious inner state as a priority.

My Cosmic Name

4th May was an auspicious day. I felt wonderful, as if a shift in consciousness had occurred. In my early morning meditation I invoked wise teachers from the highest dimensions of Love and Light and asked my Higher Self to vet whoever chose to work with me. I was then invited to travel to an incredibly high dimension and, upon accepting the invitation, saw three Beings of Light, the Elohim, pulling me up as if on a fishing line. I noticed, and was told, that I was passing by the Andromeda Galaxy.

The Light Beings asked if I would join them in their play. I questioned whether their work was for the betterment of humanity, the Earth and the galaxy. I also asked if it was according to the wish of the Prime Creator explaining I wasn't willing to play games with them if they were in any way detrimental. They assured me that all was part of the Creator's Plan and that they were creators themselves and were only interested in doing Light work through joy and play. I agreed and said I would really enjoy doing this work, and thanked them for inviting me. We joined hands to cement our agreement and then danced and played joyously.

If, during your meditations, a spiritual being invites you to participate in their service endeavours it is important to check their credentials. Ask three times if they are from the light. If, on the third time, they say no, then politely refuse their invitation and guide them into returning to their home/dimension. Universal Law states they must answer truthfully on the third time. I have found this to be true in all cases.

It was then the Elohim gave me my cosmic name, Ashtara, and asked me to adopt it.

I was surprised, and wondered about the significance of this new name. My birth name was Barbara and I had never heard the name Ashtara before. Later, I researched its numerology to find it related to the number 23/5.

The number 23 is about bringing the trinity of body/

mind/spirit into alignment through balancing the inner masculine and feminine energies. It has a mercurial component indicating the individual has a quick and agile mind and body, is gifted in speech and writing and often carries much wisdom and intelligence. Often 23's have unusual ideas that need to be presented in an entertaining fashion to have their greatest effect. Their ideas and writing can bring about positive change to the collective when well presented. Five represents the five-pointed star, the ancient symbol for the sacred feminine. This number is also indicative of change.

Once I had some idea of what was involved in the cosmic name I had been given I let go of my curiosity and accepted the idea.

Mr Squiggle

During a following meditation I was taken to a dimension of incredibly fine frequency. My heart and lungs felt the pressure however I was able to manage it. I saw rainbows and heard a sound that was like a soft 'aaahhh' floating on the breeze, and was told this was the breath of Source – peaceful, light, gentle and balanced. I saw angels and they were so happy, joyful and loving, full of fun. One kissed me gently and then the three Elohim came and asked me to think of something I'd like to play at that was fun.

I thought of a ball so they manifested a big one. Then I said I wanted to play with medium sized balls - one for each of us. So they created five balls, one for each of us, plus a spare. They threw them all into the air to make a formation like an atomic structure with one larger central sphere and the other smaller spheres circling and connecting energetically to the main one. It seemed to me they were demonstrating the atomic process of creation.

A few days later, when I experienced their playfulness again, they suggested I read about them in the bible. I did so and learned that they are creator gods who work directly with, and for, the Creative Source/God. The name Elohim means "god" or "gods" in both modern and ancient Hebrew language.

Sai Baba continued to give me transmissions about love that were particularly applicable to my life. They were beautiful heart opening words that later became my book *The Crack in the Cosmic Window*. I love that title.

During other parts of my meditative training I was encouraged to become the observer of, and identify, every sensation and emotion in my body as it arose, at all times. This applied to my every day life as well as to my meditative experiences. One of the questions I was to regularly ask of myself was "Am I feeling uplifted by this encounter, or not?" If not, then I'm to move away from it. Another was to get very clear distinctions about the cause of my hot menopausal flushes. My guides asked me to determine the parts of my body where they started. If I felt pressure first in my head then it was my guides giving me an energetic transfusion, however if the flush originated in my body then it was self-doubt arising. These, and other self-questioning exercises formed part of my discrimination training.

I was also trained to become acutely aware of negative entities from lower dimensional realms that tried to inhabit my energy field. I didn't want to be contaminated and dragged down by them as I had been by my former friend in the 3D world.

I was still experiencing relationship problems and knew

I had to find a way to rise above my emotional reactions to my husbands criticisms and judgements of me, and the people with whom I associated. Every negative word felt like a sharp barb entering my body, and I allowed the barbs to weaken my energy levels. I also found his angry outbursts difficult to handle. As mentioned previously whenever I felt emotionally upset my head felt encased in fog, and I couldn't think. I could only feel – deeply and intensely. One of the realizations I had was that in order for me to feel loving I needed to be balanced and in my own power. When I unconsciously gave my power (life force energy) away to him I become weak and nervous. To feel empowered I needed to speak the truth of my emotions and some of them were still camouflaged in my subconscious. I decided then that I must learn to identify them.

I chose to do this by writing each of the astrological zodiacal signs, with their feeling/emotional key words, on large flip charts. These I distributed around the house where altercations took place. When immersed in emotion I could then search for the appropriate word on the flip chart, identify it within me, and then verbalise it. This was the only way I knew how to connect with, and verbalise, the truth of my emotions at the time of feeling them. During this process I also learned to take responsibility for my emotions and to never use the word "you" because this inferred blame and would always result in an attacking reaction.

I was committed to our marriage and spoke to him about my issue. It was difficult to maintain peace and harmony but I did my best. It was at great energetic cost.

Somewhere around this time Mother Mary came again and this time she identified herself. As she did so I became immediately aware of a left-brain programmed thought of self-doubt containing a 'not good enough' pattern begin to take over my mind but I commanded it be silent. I allowed my right brain, the abstract and intuitive side, to take precedence. And then Mother Mary was able to access my vibratory level to speak her words of wisdom.

She told me that my vibration was like Mr Squiggle, a funny children's TV cartoon character of the time. He entertained, taught, wrote lessons and was fun, educational, different and unique. She said I was to teach, write and entertain. I loved this image, and what she said came true. Some of my students said they came to class for the entertainment value because, through the fun and mental stimulation I naturally created, they learned so much about themselves.

She then said I would be having a break from dictation because there were things going on energetically of which I was unaware. My energy levels needed to be built up again and healing needed to take place. She told me she is always available to call upon whenever I feel the need of her. I felt her sincerity, love and compassion and she was so gentle and nurturing that I relaxed and basked in her energy. She placed her hands upon my head and I immediately felt a surge of higher vibrational energy pour through me. I felt truly blessed.

A few days later I was taken by another gentle Light Being, with different energy to Mother Mary, up into space and to my left. It felt as if I was traveling around a very large sphere, way out to the left of the galaxy. When the process stopped I felt calm and incredibly peaceful. Then shapes began to appear in my inner vision and became a group of nine beings that said they were the Masters of Meaning. They invited me to ask them for answers whenever I needed to know meaning. They also said that, as I bring more meaning into my life, I would be able to express this vibration and act as a catalyst and pioneer of meaning to others.

They formed a circle and blended their energy with mine. I asked them to place their hands on my head and I could feel slight pressure on the left side of my head, as well as warmth. It felt wonderful. I then asked them to place their hands on my heart and this also felt blissful. I was calm and centred and realized how deeply loved I am by many spiritual guides.

I also learned to appreciate the value of meaning in my life. The metaphysical and spiritual teachings I was receiving helped me to understand that each soul has a specific purpose on earth. Life can become incredibly meaningful when we understand the bigger picture of our spiritual evolutionary journey and the direction of soul purpose. This purpose involves the conscious embodiment of finer frequencies of light so that a return to the light of Source can take place. During the course of many lifetime journeys we experience the by-ways and highways. Some experiences pull us off track and we implode and spiral downwards into density. We then lose track of our soul's purpose. The further down the evolutionary spiral we go the greater the struggle to regain the light of higher consciousness. The only way we can embody greater light is to connect every day with our soul through heart-felt feelings of love, joy and gratitude. This reconnection can also occur through daily meditation.

I was also learning to appreciate the energetic system that underpins the cosmos and life on earth. This system replicates, from the tiniest particle to the largest galaxy. Has anybody else ever thought that electrons spinning around the nucleus of an atom look exactly like a miniature version of planets orbiting the Sun?

Esoteric astrology is the study of cosmic energy patterns and how these forces impinge upon all within their field of influence. Our individual energy patterning also impinges upon those within our circle, our field of influence. It can be poisonous or uplifting depending upon our level of consciousness (light). Once conscious of the cause of dysfunctional programming the solution follows so we can make the necessary evolutionary changes.

I received many messages about how important it was to focus on healing myself, and to trust myself to speak my truth, especially in my marriage, and how insidious and weakening is self-doubt. I also appreciated the tremendous legion of spiritual masters who made themselves available to assist my ascension path. I realized I was the only one who could heal myself from the pain and angst I created. My guides could help me rebalance and infuse me energetically but essentially I must correct my negative patterning.

So I decided to embark on yet another healing journey to assist in becoming clear about my deep-seated psychological issues. I was aware that, once I fully understood the depths of my negative thinking and beliefs I could implement change, no matter how difficult this might be. Astrological analysis was my main healing tool. I also accessed past lives to seek cause, knowing full well that until cause of my core issue was accessed, accepted and loved, my soul 'wounds' would continue to hold poison. Eventually that poison would affect my body detrimentally and I wasn't interested in that degenerative path. I understood that, in each lifetime, our personality self is a unique one-time composite of soul fragments containing memories of times past. This is why each individual is so unique.

I believe we incarnate upon Earth to learn specific lessons so our soul can spiritually evolve into greater light and divine love. Most people learn about themselves through intimate relationships. If we do not learn our life lessons with one partner then the lessons repeat with others until we do. Eventually we develop higher consciousness and divine love through self-awareness, and by taking personal responsibility for all we feel, think and project onto others and our manifest world. This process usually takes many lifetimes. Many old souls are incarnate now who are here to complete their 3D journeys this time around, so their lessons are more intense.

One of Sai Baba's transmissions helped me on my healing journey. I share it in the hope it will support you.

"Love is joy, the spontaneous outpouring that comes from a heart overflowing with love. This joy is to be shared. When one loves oneself sufficiently the heart feels free to experience joy. Creative expression is the result. Joy comes from loving self enough to simply be and allow all forms of creativity to emerge. We are creative beings with the capacity to spread joy and love to others. First we need to discover this feeling for ourselves. The only way to discover it is to learn to love one's true essence and to honour the spark of the Divine Creator within.

Courage comes from joy. This is not the false courage of the ego wanting to be first and best. True courage is being willing to express heart-felt feelings to others without self-consciousness of any kind. This type of courage is earned by consciously working through the barriers of negativity built up around the heart. This takes courage. Joy, happiness and fulfilment are the result of this work. Love of self means loving the Divine spark within you, the spark from your Creator. Dishonouring your true essence is dishonouring your Creator. It takes courage to love self. It takes courage to break the ego's hold over your essence. However, it is from this inner work that joy comes. Joy is the result of loving yourself and the Divine spark of God/Goddess within more than anything else. Then, once the ego is quelled and the love of your Divine essence is deeply and truly felt, joy results that you can share abundantly and lovingly with others. This is true service."

Independence

As well as courage, independence was another major issue I was working on. I found it extremely difficult to consider myself equal to another so I put everyone else's feelings, ideas and opinions above my own. I loved to serve others but found it incredibly difficult to attain balance by first serving myself.

Even though I was now speaking the truth of my feelings and experiences to my husband I was still allowing invalidation. I took the blame for everything that was going wrong in our relationship. I believed my husband when he said it was my fault and did whatever I could to correct. Now, at the time of writing, I see how I projected my disowned and suppressed anger and frustration that he played out so magnificently. I can also see how I continually judged myself as wrong, so received judgement back. I learned well from my experiences and am extremely grateful for them. They helped me develop inner strength and the conviction that, although my path was different to most, it was right for me. My husband was a wonderful teacher.

A Pleiadian Experiment

During my meditation on June 14th I was taken to a spaceship and greeted very warmly by a group of little, round, one-eyed green creatures. They looked liked small and cute cartoon 'humpty-dumpty' characters. They were the same beings I had encountered previously and I felt very comfortable with them. They telepathically asked if I would allow them to do an experiment on my brain. I grilled them extensively about this request because I was unwilling to experience manipulation or control. I asked them three times if they were from the Light and they said they were. Then I quizzed each one individually as to whether they were of the Christ consciousness. I sent a red ray to each one and received it back instantly. So I agreed. (I must have been taught this red-ray practice some time previously because I did it without conscious thought). I felt they were curious, respectful and extremely perplexed by human complexity.

They placed a type of metal helmet over my head and I felt tingles on the right side. I said so and they carefully repositioned the helmet. They did the same process to the left side. After they removed the helmet they offered me a cup of green tea, as they knew I liked it. I didn't wonder where it came from. I asked where they were from and they said, "the Pleiades, and we are your brothers". I felt completely at ease with them. They then beamed me down to my platform where Sai Baba was waiting. He placed his hands on my head to give me a transfusion of love energy.

It would have been interesting to be privy to the humpty-dumpty's findings.

Another Experiment

A few days later I entered a deep meditative space and my eagle guide took me to a space ship. There I met with the little green Pleiadian 'humpty-dumpties' again. They were so cute and appealing and I loved them. Their heads and hands appeared to be disproportionately larger than their bodies. I felt their love and wasn't surprised by their features. In fact I felt as if they were part of a family I had known at another time in my soul's history.

They asked if they could put the helmet on my head again. I asked them to explain what they were doing and they said they were checking my evolutionary progress through my DNA. They said I was highly evolved and were monitoring me, along with a few others, to see just where we were 'at' in our level of consciousness. They were kind, gentle and emotionally detached. I felt they must be scientists observing and recording the evolutionary progress of selected humans, and I was part of their experiment.

As they placed the helmet I felt an ache in the lower middle back section of my head. This part of the head is where past life memories are stored and I wondered if the helmet was activating a past memory. I also experienced an uneasy feeling in the pit of my stomach. It didn't feel like fear but I couldn't identify it clearly. When they took the helmet off I asked for Sai Baba to once again place his hands on my head. I felt his loving vibration course through me and began to feel better. The little Pleiadians thanked me and said they would not need me again for quite some time.

Then I caught the eagle again and he took me to my Tall One. We danced together, waltzing at first and then danced the rock and roll. We had such fun and moved so well together. Then I was taken to a mountaintop and asked to survey the world. My Tall One said that I had climbed a symbolic spiritual mountain and now had the world at my feet. It was up to me to create my reality so I needed to become aware of my thoughts, as what I think manifests. I also needed to trust, without seeking reasons. I understood that the next step on my spiritual growth path would be a major learning curve.

Hidden Symbols

Around this time art became a hobby. One of my friends chose to hold art classes and I decided to attend. I had not been to art classes before because I was hopeless at drawing. My level of competence was that of a child and stick figures were the best I could create. I had fun drawing them though, and they amused my astrology students. The important thing was that they understood the teaching I was endeavouring to share. The crazily drawn simple stick figures helped them relax and absorb the information.

I'd always been reluctant to further the drawing process however my artist friend told me I wouldn't need to draw, only paint. Her method of teaching produced amazing results for all the students. Soon after we arrived at class she guided us into a deep relaxation and meditation. This was obviously a technique to quieten the rational left-brain to allow intuitive guidance. By the end of the six-week course I had produced six amazing works of symbolic art. I didn't understand the symbols however I realized they were based on ancient knowledge stored in my subconscious. This six-week course enabled me to trust my inner knowing more than ever before.

Transmissions on Love

During meditation on June 24th 1995 the Archangel Michael took me on a journey to visit the Planet of the Whispers. This planet was exquisitely beautiful, soft, shimmering and misty with a dream-like quality. The colours were clear, a little like a rainbow. I also observed clean and placid pools of water. The energy of the environment felt wonderful. The gentle constant rocking movement and small fairy like creatures I encountered stirred memories of a life, or lives, of being one of these gentle creatures. I was told I have these same loving and gentle qualities and that they need to surface.

Later, following descent to my meditation platform, Mother Mary came to administer and asked me to allow her love to heal. I heard and sensed angelic singing as she worked on my energy field, and then I wept healing tears. I felt so loved and nourished by her nurturing presence. She told me I have much valuable knowledge and wisdom inside me, waiting to emerge. I still find that I am deeply affected emotionally whenever anyone, especially a gentle male, offers me consideration, care and nurturing love.

I felt so much lighter and brighter the following day. During meditation I was spiralled up a long way where everything was still and peaceful. Then I heard the voice of God/Goddess say

"Focus on filling yourself with love and light many times a day. Your work is about to begin and this focus is needed. Whenever you wash your face, comb your hair and perform other simple daily tasks focus on filling yourself up. It is your fuel. Never doubt that it is I who have spoken."

The following transmission from Sai Baba emphasises the point made above.

"Love Is. It is the creative force that emanates from God/Goddess and is divine in content. Allow it to permeate every cell of your body. Feel it affecting you internally. Feel the vibration of love working to change your molecular structure. Visualize the process in your mind. Feel this loving essence from the Creative Source heal and nourish. It is your fuel and life-blood. It is the blood of the soul. Open up your hearts and allow the Creator's love to enter your being. By allowing, imagining and feeling this process there will be a change in your molecular structure. You will become lighter, more radiant and experience greater balance and calm. Transformation will take place. This process requires conscious effort and will. It also requires understanding and a belief that the process works. Focus attention on bringing this love essence into your body at every available opportunity each day. In time you will feel more loving and lighter and will then emanate these qualities. People will be attracted to you for your light and love and will feel more balanced and calm in your presence.
Love Is."

Jesus's disciple, Matthew, confirmed this message when he visited me during a meditation the following month, delivering a message from Jesus. The message was that I needed to consciously and with intent open my heart to love and vulnerability, because this is where my greatest strength lies.

The Archangels' Wings

A few days later I was taken to the light city on Sirius and greeted by my stellar family, the Sirian Council of Nine. This journey was different to other times because I did not have an eagle guide. Instead my vehicle was a particular energy formation - a mass concentration of energy in the shape of a reversed cone propelling me vertically to my destination. On Sirius I was placed on the healing crystal wall and given an energetic transfusion where I felt waves of fine currents move through me. Following the energy transfusion I descended to my 'platform' to be greeted by Sai Baba who blessed me and asked me to place my hands beneath his. I could feel his loving energy move through my hands as a very strong healing current.

Archangels Michael and Gabriel visited me during another meditation and offered to be my wings until I was able to find my own. I accepted. They had something special to show me, they said, and flew me into outer space to view millions of spacecraft encircling earth. I felt in awe at the vast numbers. It felt reassuring, as if the beings in the space ships were both monitoring and protecting Gaia, our precious planet, and all of humanity upon her.

A Bulgarian Adventure

During a meditation on 31st July 1995 I danced beautifully the Paneurythmy with its' founder, Peter Deunov. It felt amazingly light and energizing. He told me I had a karmic duty to perform associated with this dance and that it would unveil itself when the time was right.

And then, in early August, I physically travelled to

Bulgaria where the dance originated early in the 20th century. I visited this country specifically to learn and integrate the many different exercise steps. When Peter Deunov was alive he often taught this sacred circle dance in the high Bulgarian Rila Mountains. He continued teaching throughout the communist invasion knowing full well if he, and the dancers were caught, they would be killed. The group moved from mountaintop to mountaintop to avoid this possibility, often dancing in the snow and the rain. Peter Deunov trained in USA as a medical doctor, specializing in the brain. He also played the violin, the instrument he used to teach Panuerythmy. He passed away in Sophia, Bulgaria in 1944.

Bulgaria had been under occupation for three hundred years and the communists were the last invaders. They left only a few years before I journeyed there. I travelled alone and felt their controlling influence very strongly. My first experience, upon arrival at the unpainted bare concrete and steel 'prison' type airport, was of being grabbed on the back of my neck by a huge woman. She lifted me up and placed me at another counter, yelling at me in her language. Apparently all the British Airways passengers from London were required to fill in immigration forms that had not been distributed on board the aircraft. I wasn't worried by this cold and unexpected greeting rather I was amused at the images my mind created. The scene brought up memories of a James Bond movie where one of Bond's antagonists was a huge and aggressive KGB Russian woman spy. The movie character was so similar to the physical one who accosted me. How could I not smile?

In Sophia, the capital, the psychic atmosphere was as dense as at the airport. People lived in fear and oppression even though the communists had been gone for a few years. They seemed depressed, suspicious and morose. I felt so much compassion for them, and their plight.

I was very fortunate because my husband had visited this country the previous year on business. He had delivered a letter, a parcel of my books and some magazines to an English speaking Bulgarian woman I had been recommended to contact by a British friend. This woman ran a spiritual women's centre in Sophia. In my letter I explained how passionate I was about the Paneurythmy dance and asked whether she knew of anyone who could help me get to the mountains to learn more about it.

My husband told me that Minka and her friends were the warmest, most hospitable and friendly Bulgarians he had encountered during his visit and I experienced the same.

After I had passed through immigration and customs these women greeted me with warm hugs. They were most welcoming and I felt completely safe in their hands. I stayed at the Women's Centre and noticed that all the books and magazines I donated the previous year had been well read. I added to them with the greatest pleasure.

I stayed in Sophia for four days. One morning, wanting to send some postcards to Australia, I travelled by tram to the post office, a small bare, unpainted concrete and steel building where another huge KGB type woman sat behind a steel grill. I handed her twenty postcards, each with masses of writing and had to wait while she read every one. Apparently her job was to make sure I had not written any propaganda or derisive comments. However I doubted she could read English and felt her actions to be a demonstration of egotistical authority.

Before leaving Sophia to travel to the mountains where

the dancing was to take place I had to walk to another bare concrete and steel building in the centre of town. There I had to stand in line while one typist, using an old Imperial typewriter, wrote a letter detailing my travel plans. After an hour of waiting I received the letter and then had to have it checked and stamped at another counter. It was midsummer, 30 degrees centigrade, very hot and sticky and no air conditioning. Inside the building were masses of people irritated because of the lengthy delays. The staff did their best with their limited resources even though they were overwhelmed and stressed.

Armed with this precious letter I went to the next counter to again stand in line. Eventually I had my travel arrangements approved and stamped, although I did have to be assertive when another large aggressive woman jumped in the queue ahead of me as I was about to be served. I tapped her on the shoulder, spoke assertively and could see she understood every word. She was Bulgarian, living in Canada and spoke English well. She apologized profusely.

Two days later I joined a small group of people being driven, in a rickety old car, into the beautiful countryside. We were dropped at the base of the 2500 metre high mountain we were required to climb. There were no roads to the camping site so we carried our backpacks, and donkeys carried the extra luggage. Even though I intended to stay in the mountains for three weeks to learn the dance I hadn't brought many clothes because Minka had warned me that our tents would be small. Some people found the climb quite steep but I managed it well. It only took me about two hours to reach the top.

The atmosphere was so different in the mountains. It felt clean, invigorating and safe. I was warmly welcomed and shown my tent, situated on a small piece of relatively flat land directly across from another mountain range. There was a small valley separating the two ranges and, even though it was mid-summer, there was snow on the mountain on the other side of the valley, seemingly the same altitude as my tent. I realized it would be very cold at night. Because of the high altitude there was very little vegetation and the few trees around were stunted to about one metre high. However it was enough for me to create a privacy screen and allocate an area for my ablutions. I found an old rusty tin can that I used to dig my ablutions hole. I also created a washing basin with two strong plastic bags I had purposefully bought over from Australia, stringing them up between two branches.

The spring was a long way down the mountain from my tent so part of my daily schedule was to collect water to use to drink and wash. The water was pure, highly mineralised and very healthy. I discovered I was resourceful and really enjoyed the mountain challenges. After about ten days I was desperate for a shower so, with a couple of other women, I found a bucket and collected hot water from the make shift kitchen. While everyone else was dancing on another mountain we managed to have a sponge bath. It felt fantastic. Washing our hair proved more difficult and we had to go to a nearby stream to do so. The water was icy cold and my head didn't like it. I screamed, and laughed, from the sharp needle-like pain. We each managed to wash another's hair and felt so much better afterwards.

The special days for the dance were between the 19th and 21st August. During this time many hundreds, perhaps thousands, of people from all around the world assembled to practice, in concentric circles, the sacred dance. The numbers of men and women seemed to be about equal. There are seven sacred lakes in these mountains, representing the seven chakras of the human body, and we danced at whichever one would hold the number of people present. I was so pleased I had arrived early in August because I was able to experience dancing at all of the lakes. Members of the Bulgarian symphony orchestra were our musicians and they played in the centre of the concentric circles. Their violin music was exquisitely beautiful. Many of the globe trotting musicians were regular Paneurythmy dancers.

Each afternoon we would hike on picnic excursions to other mountaintops and always there would be someone playing the violin from one mountaintop or another. I felt the vibrations of the exquisitely beautiful and poignant music in every fibre of my being. The Bulgarian mountain people are as agile as goats and seemed to glide, rather than climb, these mountains.

There were two old people, one a man aged 94 and the other a women of 87, I felt very privileged to meet. Both had been Peter Deunov's students. They lived in the mountains, travelling and teaching wherever they were invited. They didn't have a home but were welcome wherever they went. They were lithe, fit and healthy.

My journey to Bulgaria was an incredibly magical time in my life and all the people involved in the Paneurythmy movement were so welcoming. I learned much about Peter Deunov's teachings, his life and the value and meaning of the dance. It completely aligns with astrology and the sacred geometric patterns formed by the planets and stars.

I had booked to stay in the mountains for three weeks but, after two weeks, it started to rain. We then danced in our boots, rather than barefoot as was required to keep our connection to Mother Earth, and in our hooded rain jackets. Eventually the rain soaked my tent and blankets so I sadly left a few days earlier than planned. On the way down the mountain I picked and ate fresh mountain raspberries. An old truck was waiting to take us, a small group of three people, back to Sophia where Minka was waiting for me at the Women's Centre.

My fond memories of the wonderful experience are of masses of people, all dressed in white with gold belts, twirling and weaving in and out of each other enjoying their mountain dance experience. The still waters of the lakes reflected the clear blue sky and the constant sound of sheep's bells added to the picturesque scene. I will never forget the exquisite sounds of violin music being played by talented musicians standing on the top of nearby mountains. Each time I think about it now I feel a warm fuzzy tingling in my heart.

Spiritual Growth Accelerates

On my return home to Australia my classes and daily meditations continued. On 4th September, during my meditation, the Archangel Michael returned, advising my spiritual growth was now to be accelerated and I am to allow, and trust, the process and completely let go of control.

This last requirement is not easy. Fear is underneath control. It takes a huge leap of faith to develop enough self-trust to enable the release of fear. However I promised myself I would do my best. It was another challenge for me to develop even greater self-awareness.

The next day Michael continued with this theme saying that I have the creative ability to visualize what I want and it would come to me. He said I could make the waters part in a lake, or the rain stop. I had apparently learned this process in the past. All I need to do is create whatever I want in my mind, and it will happen.

This seemed incomprehensible at that time. Now, at the time of writing, I look back and accept the truth of his statement. However, I needed to remind myself to make a conscious effort to activate and practice this creative ability, knowing full well the importance of operating in authenticity, integrity and love. I also know how important it is to be in complete alignment with my emotional, mental and spiritual bodies. When all these are aligned with what I want to create nothing can stop it taking place. I have always been aware of the consequences of inappropriate, non-loved based action, and the karma that would accumulate from it.

Around this time I must have also been learning from, and being guided by, Tara, the feminine Tibetan Buddha, because she is mentioned in my notes. I can't remember, nor did I record, when she started to work with me. I perceive her as very feminine and beautiful. She is beautiful - small, slight, well rounded and wears fresh flowers in her hair and beautiful jewellery on her olive skin.

A few days later I was again taken, during my meditation, to the Light City on Sirius for healing. Again the procedure was the same as described earlier. I was strapped to a clear healing wall and administered to by the Sirian Group of Nine. They told me that I now co-exist in two-dimensional worlds as apparently I had done before, in a previous existence.

Following my descent to a lower dimension Mother Mary and her assistants gave me an energy healing. I noticed they were extracting a great deal of dense grey material from my etheric body. This was sent to the light for transmutation. I could also see they used a kind of laser apparatus to seal my emotional body from energetic contamination. I thought to myself how wonderful it would be if our medicos were willing to study light and sound technology so they could use it for healing purposes. It would be a progressive step if they could develop an apparatus to cleanse, heal and seal the emotional and spiritual bodies from human psychological contamination.

I began writing short stories in early September. I was intuitively aware of my guides transmitting them and it was so easy. I loved writing the stories because each one contained a valuable message. I never knew what they would be about or how they would end. Some are very child-like however the messages are applicable to all ages. Some of these stories form my book *A Treasure Trove of Gems*. A few days later, during meditation, my guides took me to the top of a mountain where I told them I wanted to write best sellers that would inspire and enthuse readers to become the best they could be, and excite them into creating uplifting new beginnings.

I said I wanted to teach Paneurythmy around the world, and travel to global sacred sites. I also wanted to heal, have one on one contact with people, and to entertain on stage. I put in my order and all of the above, except the best seller, came true however there's still time for that.

The following month, during meditation, I was advised that, prior to my earthly incarnations I came from the stars and it is to the stars I will return. However, before

I do so I have a mission to complete, a responsibility I committed to fulfil prior to this incarnation. Astrology, Panuerythmy, creative self-expression, speaking publically and writing are all part of this mission and it is important for me not to become side tracked.

On my return to my lower frequency platform I visited my imaginary crystal cave, a special meditative place I've created where I go to experience healing and grounding. It is also where I access information. It was there I was introduced to nine crystal guardians who asked if I would work with them to ensure that the crystal balance would not be disturbed upon planet Earth. I agreed, and did my best with their commission. Here is another transmission I felt would be appropriate and useful:

"It is time for the world to know the true function of minerals and crystals and the part they play in the Earth's stability. From way back in the distant past, when our Creator, the Supreme Being, created the galaxies and the system of planets revolving around a Sun, a method was needed to solidify the movement of the planets in their orbits. There needed to be a stabilizing force, an energy that kept the planets in their correct orbiting position. So, minerals and crystals were created. They contain energy that is both electrical and magnetic. These energy components connect the minerals and crystals to a grid system deep within the Earth and create a force that holds and binds the whole system in place.

When too many minerals or crystals are taken from particular points of the grid a systems imbalance occurs. This is happening on Earth now. The planet is experiencing problems internally as well as externally. Planets are living evolving organisms with molecular structures. The understanding of how this system works is being beamed to

earth so people can become more aware of the predicament they are in and begin to address the imbalance. The seesaw is overbalancing in favour of negativity or darkness. This must be addressed, and soon".
Abraham

Zodiacal polarities

During meditation one morning the following month I was told that the next level of my training was in assertiveness. I was to learn to value myself sufficiently highly that I could express my truth with conviction, clarity and courage. When this was learned I would be able to easily materialise whatever I needed.

I was beginning to see more clearly how I create 3D reality with my thoughts. I had been a frightened and insecure adult child, struggling to gain self-understanding, purity, self-worth, self-value and self-love. It has been a long, and hard, journey. Sometimes I floundered, nearly drowning in an ocean of emotion. Yet something always drove me on. That 'something' is the spark of divinity within my soul. It walks within me every step of the way.

Learning to bring into balance my inner polarities enabled acceleration of my spiritual evolutionary progress, and the zodiacal system is the tool I used. I learned very early in my astrological studies to understand the six polarities within the twelve zodiacal signs. I imagine the twelve signs representing six different coins. Each coin has two sides. The top of one coin represents one sign and the bottom its opposite sign. Each of the signs has different characteristics and psychological manifestations. We all have the stars within, as astrophysicists have proved, so everyone plays out the zodiacal polarities, usually unconsciously and dysfunctionally. But we don't have to play our game of life this way.

Corrections can occur once we understand, and consciously work with, the system. For example in the zodiac Aries is the opposite sign to Libra. When integrating and bringing into balance, through much practice in daily life, the positive characteristics of both the signs, inner harmony and peace result. Emotional reactions no longer take place because emotional mastery, which is not suppression, has been learned and integrated. Thus negative karmic imprints can be successfully overcome through a committed and dedicated application of spiritual astrology to one's life.

I was also learning to forgive myself for my ignorance and emotional angst knowing I did the best I could with the knowledge I had at the time. I take responsibility for my astounding life creations.

The next day I experienced a re-arrangement of my DNA and was told how necessary it was to enable the next part of my training. I felt the process in my body and accepted what was said as true, but I didn't understand it. I understood that I was being trained to trust my inner guidance.

Supreme Being

On the morning of November 6th, during my early morning meditation, I felt a great deal of heat and higher frequency energy enter my crown. I then saw and felt myself to be in a rocket type vehicle traveling incredibly quickly to my left and then bursting through a star gate to access higher dimensions. I travelled on in multitudinous energy waves beyond the speed of light and then encountered the Supreme Creator who asked me to continue my dedicated spiritual practices and service and then the task would be given.

A few days later I was engaged in the meditative practice whereby I imagine I am ascending twelve steps. During this practice my mind is completely blank and I have no agenda. I totally trust. I was guided to ascend to the twenty-third step being advised along the way that the numbers at this level become energy and vibration. As I travelled up the vibrating numbers there appeared to be many luminous beings blessing me and forming an over-arcing tunnel of light. They were chanting the sacred sound of AOM and it felt special. The energetic resonance from their combined chanting entered my body and I felt it vibrating. One Light Being, moving in front of me, placed his hands upon my head. I was told this ceremony was an initiation and that I was deemed ready because my heart was open and my devotion pure. I needed to be patient and follow my heart-felt feelings because this is the way my guides work through me. I was asked to relax and enjoy life.

The next day I was taken to the star system of Vega, in a chariot. The colours there were very clear and luminous and the energy felt wonderful. I was asked to rest there to enable restorative balance.

Pleiadian Message

In the 3D world my first public teaching of the Paneurythmy dance took place on 24th November at a spiritual healing centre one hour's drive from my home. It was a wonderful experience. Following it I was intuitively guided to connect the energy grids between Bulgaria, where the dance originated, and Australia.

And then a few days later, during meditation, I received a message from Andromeda, Theta and Beta, the names given to me for the three little humpty-dumpty Pleiadians. Opening their tiny arms in a gesture of peace, with infinite love emanating from their eyes, they told me how concerned they are about what we humans are doing to our planet. They said they have come to do what they can to help alleviate the destruction likely to occur should we continue with our ways, and that they come in love (their tiny hands were on their hearts as they spoke these words) to help restore Mother Earth to her former beauty and perfection. Their desire is to help redress the devastation man has caused. They also said that Mother Earth was in the process of shedding her skin of negativity. I felt their dedication, sincerity and love and believed all they said to be true.

Optimum Health

The message I received on the last day of November 1995 related to the importance of sound and toning, especially the chanting of the sacred sound of AOM. This sound, when chanted regularly with devotion, opens portals into other dimensions. This then allows higher vibrational energy to be easily accessed.

The second part of the transmission concerned the physical health of the human body and is extremely important.

"The physical body is only as good as the thoughts that go into it. If you program yourself to only have positive thoughts, not only about your body but also about everything in your life, then your body will always remain in a healthy state. The opposite is also true. When you see a sick person you can know for sure they have a negative thought program running about themselves. It is that simple. This is a message that needs to be broadcast, as it is of such importance. When people re-program their minds to always think positive thoughts they naturally distribute and spread this positivity. Mother Earth receives it. This uplifting energy becomes a healing tool. It starts when one individual is dedicated to this process then it grows and grows. We ask you to present this simple message to as many people as you can. The application of it to their lives will heal them and also bring healing to Mother Earth."

The Role of Light Beings

The following transmission is also important because it explains the role of the Light Beings. I wrote all the transmissions as I heard them.

"We are Beings of Light from a higher plane of existence in a form that some people are able to see but most cannot. We have evolved to a greater understanding of ourselves and of the energy system of our Creator's Plan. We recognize the magnitude and the simplicity of the order and system and work with it. Most humans work against the system purely through lack of knowledge. The knowledge of how this system works is gradually becoming known and understood by many more people on Earth. More and more people are becoming aware of the energy currents that move through them and are

able to act appropriately with them. Sometimes the energetic influences can be quite overpowering and create disharmony. This is simply because that individual is unaware of true essence and is blocking, albeit unconsciously, the positive energy flow. Self-awareness, self-understanding and one's usage of energy are the keys to alleviating feelings of heaviness or darkness.

When able to understand one's true nature and observe self as an objective 'watcher', then, and only then, can the understanding of personal energy usage emerge from the subconscious into every-day consciousness. This practice requires a detachment of the ego.

Many people are too involved in their egoic pursuits to allow this manifestation. New patterns of awareness need space in which to function and operate successfully. First there needs to be an acceptance that what individuals are doing with their life is simply not working and for them to come to the conclusion that something new needs to be tried. The old ego ways only bring frustration and unhappiness. An acceptance of this fact needs to take place before the shift into new energy patterns of thought can emerge.

Each individual will learn this truth at some time during his or her evolutionary life cycle. Many are in the process of 'waking up' and some have already awakened. It won't be too long before critical mass occurs.

Our role as Light Beings is to assist this awakening process. We help to provide individuals with circumstances that will allow them to come into understanding of their defensive patterning. Some are much more stubborn than others and do not want to look at themselves. These people will need greater shaking up if it is their souls' purpose this incarnation to experience awakening. These are the ones we assist as they each have a specific role to play in the New

Age. They are needed, just as every piece of a jigsaw puzzle is needed to complete the picture. They are to have their awakening in order for the fulfilment of the Plan.

As you can see our task is large, however there are great numbers of us willing to serve humankind in this way and it is through our love for the Creator that we willingly and lovingly carry out this mission.

Those awakened souls make our service work much easier as their lighter and loving energy helps to awaken others.

Energy works on a different level to the human form. Human form is third dimensional. The energy we refer to comes from higher dimensions. Huge amounts of energy, on different wave bands co-exist in the same space. If you can conceive the idea that you as a human contain energy and we as Beings of Light contain energy and that all the energy comes from the one Source, our Prime Creator, then you can begin to understand how the system works. If you can understand that humans are energy, with form, and we are energy without form then the concept becomes clear.

We leave you now and ask you to type and circulate this information. We will guide you. Trust and believe totally in the information contained herein. It is the truth."

Pegasus, the Cosmic Horse

During an early morning meditation on 7th December I was introduced to another form of space travel. This was via the cosmic winged white horse, Pegasus. I was asked to jump on his back and take charge of my destiny. I aimed at the shortest and most direct path home to Source and committed to fulfilling my earthly task asking that this path be revealed to me. I was advised this would soon take place and then all the pieces of the jigsaw puzzle would fit into place. Expanding my knowledge of astrology, especially esoteric astrology, was essential to this task.

I enjoyed my ride on Pegasus. He travelled very fast and the route appeared direct. I was extremely focused, observing and feeling all I could on the journey. I had fun, and it felt so exhilarating. Pegasus and I became great friends and he carried me to many different star systems. The 12th December journey took me to an incredibly beautiful area filled with brilliant lights. There I was invited to sit in the centre of a circle surrounded by a group of very loving light beings. Their message was:

"We are all merged together in light and love to demonstrate to you the feeling and the sense this process generates. We are all connected by energy, and this merging of energies through light and love acts as a binding glue. As you can see we all look like one bright ball of light yet we are separate. You are in the centre and we surround you. This feeling of oneness with everything is what we wanted you to experience this day. When an individual's light is bright enough they can merge and become one with others of light. This is often what we see transpiring during group meditations. This feeling and sense of oneness is developing on planet Earth as more and more people become lighter in their energy fields. Healing takes place this way. You will remember this. It is a good tool to use with group situations. We love, support and honour you."

They then showed me how each one is an individual light and how the group becomes one when their individual energies connect, through love. This enables unity and oneness. Healing takes place in this sacred space of love.

A few days later I was asked to imagine I had wings, was incredibly light and able to fly freely. Feeling movement under my wings I was taken into different dimensions of space. I could see buildings and fields and then noticed that Earth was becoming smaller. I felt I entered the gravitational pull of Jupiter where I was met by six different groups of spiritual masters. I continued on, feeling the pull on my body against the wings becoming heavier with pressure. I saw mists and clouds and then brilliant clear vibrant colours, like the colours of a rainbow that had no beginning and no end. The colours were all around me, lighting me up. I was part of them, and they me. I melted into them, as one.

I saw a mountaintop shrouded in clear blue light and this light appeared ethereal, soft and shimmering. It felt incredibly inviting so I flew to merge with this gorgeous soft blue light and, as I did so, a soothing, calm sensation washed over me. I moved through the blue mist and saw, seated in a circle on the top of the mountain, a group of light beings who shimmered and radiated a silvery light, as if they glowed. This glow appeared to merge so that sometimes they appeared as individual lights and, at other times, as one brilliant light. Their presence felt very stabilising and I felt incredible peace emanating from them.

They asked me to draw closer into the centre of the circle so I could feel and experience. And to close my inner eyes when I did so. I felt warmth, joy and peace develop within me and felt completely protected, respected, loved and honoured. Tears streamed down my face. I had never before experienced such profound respect, honouring and love.

I was asked to remember this joy and happiness and to recreate it whenever I needed balancing.

The Structure and Form of Creation

During my early morning walks in nature I often feel and see 'light' images being downloaded into my mind. I mentally 'grasp' these images so I can make sense of them. I am naturally curious, with an untrained scientific mind that seeks to know and understand the workings of God's creation and the place we humans play in it. I know we humans are here on Earth to evolve into greater light, the light of higher consciousness, and to open our hearts to the high frequency of divine love. At our present level of consciousness we are like kindergarten children playing, and fighting over, our toys. This is gradually changing as more and more people wake up to truth.

One early morning during my walk I imagined the universe as a transparent sphere made of masses of perfectly formed diamond shaped pieces of crystals. There are spheres within spheres within spheres and this creates a hologram with each one of its pieces forming part of the whole. I then imagined this sphere spinning through space, rotating on its axis. As diamond-shaped pieces catch the light of a Sun they sparkle with brilliance. The part of the hologram that has been lit is awakened and energized.

I imagine every human soul is likened to one of these diamond pieces.

When humans experience the light activation they begin to awaken from a dream-like unconscious state of being. The timing of this awakening is dictated by the soul before incarnation and activated by the planets, living evolving organisms, in our solar system. The transiting planets trigger specific storage points, containing soul memories, in each individual's energy field and this process is experienced as urges. Each individual unconsciously acts upon their urges according to their programmed psychological patterning. The birth chart is a model of an individual's unique energy field and each placement in the chart can be likened to an acupressure point in the meridian system of that person's field. The 'awakening' experience may not be pleasant because old dense self-destructive beliefs, attitudes and behaviour need to change to enable the embodiment of greater light and love.

An activated and awakened human has a specific role to play in the evolutionary game of life on Earth while at the same time staying connected to the hologram. The role involves the process of consciously developing and embodying greater light, the light of self-awareness and higher consciousness. During the Age of Aquarius many souls are programmed to awaken. Their evolutionary purpose will be triggered because their soul is ready for change and metamorphosis. When the evolutionary light game is over all parts return to the hologram (God/Goddess/All That Is).

The greatest source of Light in our solar system is the Sun around which planets orbit. Each atom, cell, human and planet can be likened to an individual hologram. Each solar system is an individual hologram. Each galaxy is a hologram. The force behind all life on Earth is the Sun. Within each solar system there is a Sun. Within each Galaxy there is a central Star. The Source of all creation is brilliant Light and infinite Love. From this huge Source of dynamic living light many Suns were created as sub-stations to receive the force and radiation of the Light of Source. There are infinite Suns. The planets and galaxies move in their orbits through their sector of space to the tune of celestial music. Sound is the precipitating factor to move the holograms into strategic positions to catch the Light of their particular Sun at a specific time according to evolutionary purpose.

I love my walks in nature every morning because I allow my mind and senses to become absorbed in the incredible beauty around me. I particularly enjoy nature's freshness after rain. It is often when I am completely absorbed in the beauty of flowering trees and plants, and their scents, that I receive revealing downloads. I believe it is because my heart is open and full of gratitude that my frequency rises sufficiently to enable this experience.

PART THREE

HISTORY REVEALED
1996 - 1998

The Comet

During an early morning January meditation I climbed a huge mountain and sat on the summit, hoping a spiritual being would appear. No one came. So I decided to climb another, much higher mountain. From this higher perspective I saw a comet moving directly towards planet Earth. It was very bright and seemed to be hurtling through space. Earth appeared to be wobbling on its axis more than it should. The purpose of this comet, I was told, was to 'fire' people up and awaken them into greater spiritual understanding. Its energy acted as a 'wake up' call. Apparently it was the cosmic timing for some individuals to experience an evolutionary shift, a leap forward into higher consciousness.

And then, on January 10th 1996 I received another transmission from Sai Baba:

"It is all about love. The whole process mankind is experiencing is to do with love. Love is what makes the world go round, literally. It was through love the universe

was formed. It was through love creation occurred and it is through love that evolution occurs. Love is the key.

Our Creator loves us so much and prays we will become self-realized. Mankind created the fall from Grace. This is not something the Creator intended. The fall from grace resulted in a decline, or a fall into a darker, more dense vibration where the Creator's light is blocked and seems inaccessible to many.

It was human error that created the descent into darkness and it is through human correction that ascent occurs. It is up to each individual to choose whether they wish to ascend to regain their connection to God/Goddess or whether they want to continue their descent. Free will is the principle involved and, because the Creator is pure love then he/she will not take free will away from humans. So, at some stage in each individual's life a choice is made, for ascent or descent. If ascent, and the commitment sincerely felt, then help is always at hand from the spiritual realms. Life's lessons are presented so that greater self-awareness and self-understanding is gained. This leads to wisdom.

As lower vibratory negative patterns are cleared from the human psyche a space is left for light to enter. Eventually all the darker aspects are cleared. This results in a balanced, calm, loving and centred state of being. It is from this place individuals begin to work with the Creator's Plan. The process becomes one of consciously co-creating with the Supreme Creator.

When all the inner darkness is transmuted into light there is no need to incarnate again unless the choice to do so is for a specific purpose. The spiritual Masters such as Jesus, Buddha and Krishna incarnated by choice for a special purpose, to introduce humans to the principles of love, wisdom and truth.

As always, it is up to each individual to choose the path

they take, to descend or ascend, to clear karmic debris or to create more darkness and so incur more karma."

This transmission helped me to understand how love is the highest attainable human vibratory pattern. This was clearly demonstrated by Dr Masuru Emoto when he showed how thoughts and emotions have an effect on water. He froze water from polluted streams and the shapes formed were ugly. He did the same with clean water infused with negative human thoughts. Again the shapes were ugly and malformed. However, when he froze clean water infused by human thoughts and feelings of love the patterns formed were incredibly beautiful. Our bodies are composed of a high percentage of water and our blood is a watery substance. When our emotions and thoughts are consistently loving and generous beautiful patterns form within our blood and can be seen by medical intuitives. Such a gifted person, a psychically attuned friend who lives in Sedona, USA saw diamond shapes within my blood. She told me she had never seen such a thing before.

The Spiritual Hierarchy

I received another pertinent transmission on January 24th and felt it important to include in this story.

"We of the Hierarchy are here to help in the evolution of humankind. Our role can be likened to administrators. We organize all the pieces and fit them together to make a whole. Our plan is for each individual to learn personal responsibility, that is, responsibility for how one feels, thinks and acts. Through self-awareness choices can be consciously

made which we hope will be for good. As more and more individuals reach this state of awareness, accepting personal responsibility for them selves and the lives they have created, the Plan can work with greater effect.

Balance and harmony must be restored to planet Earth. And this can only come about by individuals first finding this balance and harmony within themselves. To one's own loving self be true. If all humans really understood this and practiced it a greater degree of harmony would exist within and without.

Life is a journey towards self-realization or self-evolvement. If each soul consciously chooses this pathway then each lifetime brings us closer to this goal. Self-evolvement means evolving back to the Source from which we came, the Creative Force, or God/Goddess. Each one of us is a spark of Source and self-realization brings this awareness."

A Space Craft

During a meditation on Australia Day, 26th January 1996, I was taken to a spiritual mountaintop by two winged Light beings and asked to use my wings. Then I was invited to express what it felt like. I said that I felt nothing, no pressure and no wind. It was as if I was floating into and through nothing. Back on the top of the mountain I was asked, "What do you see?"

I looked and saw the solar system planets, and then Pluto attracted my attention. I know the planets as inner archetypal forces and Pluto felt like an angry volcano in need of expression and release. I was asked to view further. I saw Uranus sending sparks of electrical currents to Pluto provoking and prodding agitation in him. My rational brain kicked into gear at this point because I realized transiting Uranus was currently activating my birth chart Pluto. I view a birth chart as a blue print for the soul's journey to the light of conscious self-awareness. The transiting (travelling) planets activate soul memory storage chambers resident within certain areas of the human energy field. These storage chambers can be likened to acupressure points. When activated, old unconscious memories arise, in the form of emotions and motivations. I use the analogy of acupuncture needles. These needles, specifically placed into certain storage points in the body, activate emotional release.

I felt Pluto's spewing energy would be relatively easy for me to manage because I was becoming used to purposeful emotional release. The incessant prodding from Uranus, that felt like electrical charges coming from a red-hot poker, was going to get too much for Pluto and he would eventually 'blow'.

I was then asked to look closer. I saw Jupiter working hard to catch up to Saturn. Saturn was focusing on building a firm foundation and providing a solid base so that, when Jupiter met up with him, sustainable spiritual growth, optimism and expansive experiences could take place. I was then asked to view the planets from this perspective and advised that I have the knowledge, from personal experience, of the human condition. I was now to see it from a planetary perspective.

I realized then how fortunate I was to be taught astrology during some of my meditations.

A few days later, on 31st January, I was again taken, this time by the two archangels, to a high mountaintop. They asked me to look into the sky and remote view. I saw a faint, regular, flashing light coming closer and closer. It was not large and approached me gently. I found the higher frequency energy a bit heady and had to focus on my solar plexus a couple of times during the waiting period to enable me to centre. The light turned out to be a spacecraft and I was asked if I wanted to go on board. I questioned as to whether the beings on board were operating in love and light and from the Christ consciousness. I was told they were. I asked the two archangels to come with me.

As soon as we went on board I felt an incredible amount of love surround me. There appeared to be no one else in the craft. I felt a vast sense of space even though the craft had looked small from the outside. I experienced wave upon wave of love wash over and through me. The space filled with a soft pink glow, the colour of unconditional love.

I moved into another room where female light beings were seated in a semi-circle around one large desk working on their individual computers. They were semi-luminous and slightly blue. As I entered their space they turned towards me with a warm, friendly welcome. I felt so much unconditional love emanate from them that my heart opened. They were tall and slim and dressed in very sleek well-fitted body suit type outfits the material of which seemed to move as they did. The body suits enhanced their elegance and beauty. I intuited they were androgynous but had chosen to adopt a feminine form. I very much enjoyed my experience on this space ship, feeling completely comfortable and at home. I never questioned as to why the experience took place because it felt right and natural.

Meeting with Jesus/Sananda

Then on 26th March Jesus/ Sananda came into my meditation. Sananda is another name for the ascended biblical Jesus. He said that he was to be my next guide and I instantly felt over-awed and inferior. Feeling my anxiety, he asked me to maintain calm and balance otherwise he would not be able to access me. I felt tremendous waves of love coming from him, especially through his eyes and heart. The love vibration he emanated was almost overwhelming. I felt I must kneel in front of him but he wouldn't allow it. He placed my hands on his heart and his on mine, and I felt his love transference to be incredibly pure and uplifting. It was bliss. He said that I was now ready to begin working with the Christ Consciousness vibration. The steps he gave me to enable access to this higher frequency state of being were:

First I was to access my heart space and maintain access. To do so I needed to consciously create daily feelings of love, joy and lightness of spirit.

Second, I was to always speak my truth, about what I love, what gives me joy and how I truly feel in every situation. In other words - be true to me. This combined process, he said, results in a clear spiritual connection and the light of greater intelligence.

At the conclusion of this meditation I felt I needed to rest and integrate the experience. Normally I would simply write it down and then get on with my fulfilling and busy 3D life, however this was different. The deep connection I had with Jesus obviously stirred soul memories along with an incredible feeling of love and peace. I felt so grateful he had chosen to teach and guide me.

Saturn and Chiron

Towards the end of April I was taken again to the mountaintop to view the solar system planets and the cosmos. I observed Earth's wobble and it didn't appear to be as great as I had seen previously. The same comet I had seen before appeared to be attempting to fit into place at approximately a 45-degree angle. I was shown Saturn and the seven rings around it and was told that the seven rings represent seven levels of our earthly evolutionary experience. They also indicate that everything in our 3D lives is cyclic such as time, money and experiences.

This teaching completely resonated with me and I spent many happy hours studying, reflecting and analysing my life cycles, according to the astrological model, to find amazing accuracy and detail. I taught my students to do the same. It's as if a greater force is constantly present, managing the cosmic system with the purpose of providing appropriate energy channels for humans to evolve consciously into higher frequencies of light and love.

I realized how the planets act as power stations for Source. Each planet receives, stores and transmits a specific and unique package of energy. The transiting planets, on a cyclical basis, activate specific energetic storage points in the human etheric body. This activates soul memories. The timing of the activation is according to the individual's birth chart.

Should the individual choose to move forward consciously, in a positive, uplifting and loving direction, according to their soul's purpose, the journey to enlightenment proceeds easily. We have the free will to go with the planetary prompts or not. Obviously it helps to become conscious of them in order to make well-considered decisions. There are seven main levels to our spiral into higher consciousness and all levels are cyclic. At this time in human spiritual evolution many souls have been programmed to awaken from their dream-like 3D sleep to realize there is another world available, a world governed by higher consciousness and divine love.

I was then guided to view Chiron, a cosmic body in our solar system situated between Saturn and Uranus and discovered in November 1977. The myth of Chiron, the centaur, best describes his archetypal function in the astrological model. He was an astrologer, natural healer, teacher, oracle and spiritual guide. He was a wounded healer able to heal the wounds of humanity but not his own. His physical wound was to his left, feminine, side. This symbolises the wound of the human collective feminine who has been subservient to the masculine for thousands of years. The feminine allowed this wounding. The Age of Aquarius is the time when this imbalance will be corrected.

Since Chiron's discovery natural healing modalities and spiritual teachings and practices have increased. Many more women have come into power enabling positive change to our planet. Many women leaders have emulated the masculine power games while others have focused on developing love-based feminine intuitive power. There needs to be a balance whereby the intuitive and loving inner feminine guides and leads the inner masculine. This applies to the individual as well as the collective.

Chiron had a gleeful look on his face when I encountered him in my meditation. He told me his energetic role is that of opening doors of self-awareness in our psyche. Because of his positioning between Saturn and Uranus he receives, stores and transmits both their energies. When connecting to energy storage points in an individual's birth chart Chiron can bring up subconscious fears (Saturn) as we face our soul wounds. He can also activate nervous and electrical energy (Uranus) that affects our nervous system.

The planets act as mythical archetypal forces within the human psyche and Chiron and I have had many adventures together. His energy assisted me in opening many locked doors in my psyche to enable greater self-awareness. When this awareness is applied to daily life, usually through correction of formerly unconscious habitual patterning, lightness of being results.

A few days later I was again taken into space to view the same comet and noticed it had settled. Apparently its force had temporarily interfered with the Earth's wobble. I realized how necessary it is for Mother Earth to regulate her balance otherwise there would be catastrophic solar system upheaval. To avoid this catastrophe the collective human consciousness must come into balance. Every individual who chooses to embark upon the spiritual journey to higher consciousness aids the process. I quote from another transmission. I didn't record the transmitters name.

"Balance is the key. At this time it is more important than ever before for humans to learn to create internal balance. Once this happens the energy of that balance radiates to Earth and helps to overcome her imbalance."

The Path of Self Love

Early May Transmission:

"It is time for more information. The more light and love you bring into your hearts the more your darkness will dissipate. Light always heals darkness. Light is information and knowledge. Darkness is ignorance and fear. 'To Thine Own Loving Self Be True' is all each person is here to do and be. This is their path. We are disappointed that so many people are in denial of their true selves; however that is their choice and we honour them for it.

Earth is a learning place for humans to feel sensations, feelings and emotions. No other planet has this same energy. However, too much emotional negativity has created an imbalance in Earth's energy field. It has become too dense with unresolved emotions. Steps need to be taken. Those individuals who are willing to face, and take responsibility for, their emotional negativity will move through the veil of illusionary life into a different sphere of consciousness. Others will stay behind. This is a personal choice."

Universal Design Patterns

Towards the end of April Archangels Gabriel and Uriel took me into infinite space, to visit Source. I was asked to notice the universal design patterns. I saw many packages of light in snowflake design, all of different bright, clear and vivid colours. I felt extreme bliss because this creation was so amazingly beautiful yet so simple.

I've since seen this same design photographed and displayed in one of Dr Masuru Emoto's books and to me it demonstrates conclusively that our universe was created by love, and that love is omnipresent.

The following month Archangels Uriel and Gabriel took me to another mountaintop where I was asked to look down to view the suffering of people on Earth. I saw so much violence fuelled by anger, greed, abuse, righteousness and hatred. I also viewed confusion, hunger and emotional angst. I felt the plight of humanity so intensely that my heart hurt. The message received was that I was to help heal these people. However, I may need to sacrifice my emotional attachment to my family in order to assist the family of man, and this is what I incarnated to do.

Speaking the Truth

Another strong message came through elaborating on how important it was to speak my truth, no matter how strange it might appear to others. My guides said this was a prerequisite to my major work on Earth. As I speak my truth it allows others the freedom to speak theirs.

Speaking the truth of my feelings and knowing has always been difficult so I've tended to keep it to myself. I was brought up to say what other people wanted to hear, to please them in order to "keep the peace". I was born being very sensitive to other people's emotions and energy fields and the "pleasing" game hugely influenced my life and was the source of great difficulty in my marriage. It took constant self-awareness, persistence and determination to break this old pattern.

When I first started studying astrology I read of an experimental research study conducted by a group of USA researchers. Four hundred terminally ill cancer patients diagnosed with three months to live were asked to partake in an experiment. All agreed. Psychologists must have been involved because they interviewed each patient to ascertain if there was one particular negative psychological pattern shared by all. There was, and it was the 'pleasing' game. The patients were asked if they would be willing to change this weakening habit. They had nothing to lose, and possibly something to gain, so all agreed. 90% of the patients healed their own cancer when they regularly practiced saying "no" to domineering others, and instead chose to do, and say, what was best for them. The other 10% were unable to change so passed away within the diagnosed time.

I personally experienced this same theme through a friend who had developed cancer. I visited her six days a week for over three months to give her Reiki and other forms of spiritual healing and, sometime during the course of these visits, she asked me to read her astrology chart. I did and could see that she suppressed her truth and felt unable to say "No" to her domineering and selfish husband. I told her about the cancer research and asked if she could generate the courage to confront her husband by speaking up for what she wanted and needed.

She was unable to do so. I witnessed her body blow up like a balloon and turn bright red because of the dense suppressed anger and frustration that ate into her organs. She passed away two months later, aged forty-nine. However, three days before she passed she told her husband that she wanted to be cremated and her ashes distributed over a specific mountain summit. Prior to this conversation he told her he had already bought her coffin, and his, and when she said "No" was shocked. I was so proud of her to have been able to change her habitual state of powerlessness into one of strength, even though she gave her life to do so. Her soul would have rejoiced.

A Treasure Chest

Close to my July birthday, and during an early morning meditation, the Archangel Raphael took me into a cave where I discovered a large treasure chest. I was asked to open this intriguing chest and take out the treasure, a sacred scroll and book. Attached to the book were a gold heart and a small gold chain. This book contains the history of my incarnations and is my soul's story and I have access to it whenever I want. The scroll was a certificate to say I had passed through my karmic challenges and had now graduated to a higher level of light. I was asked to always wear this symbolic golden heart next to my physical heart.

At this stage of my life I was teaching weekly spiritual astrology classes, writing articles and stories, teaching Paneurythmy and doing energy healings for people, distant as well as face to face. Many people requested astrological readings and I was happy to help them. I was also gathering a large collection of astrology books for my library, working on myself through my natal chart with each one of them. My life was fulfilling and busy.

I was able to integrate my meditation experiences into my daily life easily because they seemed so natural. I completely resonated with the higher dimensional realms, feeling 'at home' with the experiences. It was as if I knew that life well. I shared some experiences and teachings with my husband and students. Writing about them in my journal each day was a necessary grounding process and I made no attempt to remember, or reflect upon, them. Somehow I knew I would be sharing them publically when the time was right.

Gaia's Pain

During meditation on 21st November Uriel and Gabriel took me to view Mother Earth, Gaia, from space. My heart went out to her because she seemed to be struggling terribly. I felt her pain and observed her trying to free herself from heavy old 'skin'. It looked like a large eggshell was being broken open from within by a soon to be born 'baby'. I could see and feel the embryo struggling to break through the hard shell. It was awe inspiring to observe and I felt very privileged to do so.

And then on 22nd November Peter Deunov entered my meditative space to ask that I keep practicing and teaching the sacred circle dance Paneurythmy because it was helping to open my heart even more, as well as those who danced with me. He said the dance was also a vehicle for bringing into balance the feminine and masculine energies within each dancer.

December brought another visit into space where I was asked to view how both the space ships and the celestial beings were all working together to help bring stabilization and peace to Earth. On another morning I was taken through inter dimensional portals to view the Hale Bopp comet. It appeared to be on a mission and I felt its consciousness as purposeful and determined. I also observed "sucker" craft attached to its energy field.

On 24th December 1996 the two Archangels took me way out into space. I travelled through wave after wave band of beautiful colours, mostly pink and blue. We stopped at a 'space station' to view the comet again and it seemed to be more peaceful than before, not quite so hell bent on its mission. I sensed it had accomplished the main part and knew it could cruise for a while. A rosy, orange glow surrounded it. I sensed a shadow of another shape, maybe a space ship, hovering over it, but this was unclear.

I was then taken higher through wave bands of violet and silver. I saw Gaia shedding her heavy and dense 'skin' and then the old skin transmuted into light. She looked rosy and glowing just as a mother does after giving birth to a baby. I was told that I had played a small part in this "birth".

1997 - Tara

Early into the New Year I learned there is an asteroid named Tara so I placed her in my birth chart. As I did so I felt a wave of heat descend into my body through my crown and, when I closed my eyes to absorb the warmth, heard the words" I am here for you – pray and I will come". Using the same creative visualization process of invoking the planets I had been taught years ago I started working with her astrologically. Upon my invocation she entered my psychic space saying that her Taurus role in my chart was to activate a greater sense of self-worth and self-value, and to help me uncover and use my natural talents. She also said she would assist me in communicating from my heart and right brain.

This felt like a gift from heaven because I was still having problems communicating the truth of my feelings and knowing to my husband. Whenever I went into an emotionally upset space my head felt clouded by fog. I couldn't think clearly, nor could I speak properly. It was as if the dense mist from my suppressed and unidentified emotions went straight to my brain. I felt I needed to learn to identify and feel each emotion and consciously rise above each one so I could detach from them, otherwise I might 'lose' my mind. I knew I needed to train myself to observe each emotion as I felt it arise, thank it for sharing as I felt it, acknowledge and love it for its teaching, and not allow it to consume me. When I teach this process I refer to it as emotional mastery.

I realized that other people might experience a similar emotional mist in their brain so decided to include meditations, group healing and creative visualizations in my 1997 astrology classes. I feel such compassion for sufferers of mental health problems because I understand that most of their problems stem from emotional ignorance and suppression.

A few weeks later, during meditation, Ascended Master Tara came to me saying she would become a regular guide. I was happy she chose to be one of my spiritual guides because I had already done research on her and mentioned her earlier. She was Tara, the Tibetan female Buddha.

My perception of her was that of a small, well-rounded beautiful woman wearing bangles on her olive skinned arms. She wore sparkling necklaces around her throat and beautifully scented flowers in her long dark hair. She felt serene and wise. Tara asked me to keep on chanting and toning because it would help to clear my chakras from dense energetic accumulation.

I felt grateful to have two representations of Tara working with me on different dimensional realms and realized it must be time to embrace more of my feminine nature.

The Sirian Connection

On 16th January 1997 Archangels Uriel and Gabriel again entered my meditational space and took me quickly through an inter-dimensional portal. I felt as if we were birds flying lightly together on a mission. We did a large loop and then returned to our trajectory where I was asked to view.

I saw millions of stars seemingly moving in formation however the stars soon became space ships and were travelling behind comet Hale-Bopp. It felt as if they were on a purposeful mission. I noticed Earth down to the left, re-adjusting her alignment. Then I became aware of a light being in front of me, a female extra-terrestrial with very large and loving almond shaped eyes. I felt a very strong soul connection and was told she was from Sirius. Instinctively we moved our hands together in what I sensed was a universal greeting, palms vertically upright and touching each other.

I heard the Archangels say, "It is done" and the Sirian female faded back into her dimension. I was asked how my heart was feeling and I said that it was not fearful. Then I felt the transference of a warm wash of love-juice and sensed, and felt, my heart glow. I was taken back to my meditative platform/ station.

In my 3D life I attended an astrological conference and a day workshop with a USA astrologer. Surprise, surprise – on her desk was a small statue of Tara. This made me realize I could purchase one for myself. Tara's were coming at me from all angles. The workshop was great and I enjoyed it immensely.

A couple of months later, in meditation, Archangels Uriel and Gabriel took me through a portal to the left and then up vertically to view the comet and the armada of space ships again. I was beamed into one of the space ship to meet a Commander Korton who welcomed us, saying we would meet again at a later time. We moved to the back of the ship passing under a sound or light wave beam. We had to bob our heads when going under this wide beam because it felt like a force field of pulsating waves of energy. It wasn't visible. We passed into a huge area, almost like a self-contained city, where seemingly hundreds of star beings were living ordinary lives, calm, connected and happy. I understood the space ships were created of material that was way beyond our third dimensional understanding. They felt solid and secure yet seemed to expand according to purity of intent.

I was taken up to view space on a few more occasions and was told I was being trained for this task. Years later I discovered that NASA pays enormous salaries to train people to 'remote view' and then uses them for spying and knowledge gathering purposes. At least when I read those words I now have an understanding of my training, and it had nothing to do with spying.

USA Astrological Conference

In mid- March I travelled to USA to attend an astrological conference, visit my son and his family, my daughter and her partner, and a friend. I was disappointed in the conference because there was only one speaker with whom I resonated and felt a connection. However I attended as many lectures as possible; learned what I could and enjoyed my time with my family and friend.

Back home in Australia I resumed my meditation

practices and, in mid April was taken to view the comet again. It appeared to be cruising. Then I was again asked to go on board a spacecraft. I didn't record whether it was the same one as before. All the star beings were celebrating because their mission had been accomplished. They said there were now enough people on Earth embracing a more spiritual perspective to life and that the dense psychological energy of the collective human consciousness had lightened. The horrific destruction on Earth would now not occur to the degree that was probable because enough people had become open, self-aware and conscious of their spiritual nature. This was the reason behind the celebration.

Soon, I was told, the Council would need to decide the next step of the human evolutionary journey but for now it was time to rejoice. I was invited to join the fun and experienced joy, laughter, relief and lots of 'high fives' with one and two hands. I was thanked for the part I had played in the mission.

In May 1997 my guides told me that my intuitive sense about Uluru (Ayers Rock) being an energetic opening, an Earth chakra, was correct and that it was in fact a portal to underground light cities. The huge monolith rock, near the centre of Australia, forms a physical barrier to prevent humans from entering the light cities. This portal sends out powerful healing energy.

Galactic Council Meeting

During a special meditation in June I was taken to a galactic council meeting where the illumined members asked me to sit at the right hand side of their leader, at the top of a horseshoe formation. I was honoured by the group and given three gifts: a crown of flowers, a sceptre and a book of wisdom. The crown of flowers symbolized my crowning by the nature spirits and the sceptre symbolized the coming into my personal power. The book was a book of wisdom I could open anytime I wanted to know anything because all answers were contained within it.

I was asked if I would record the information being given through my experiences and I agreed. The galactic Council said that I had successfully navigated my inner murky emotional waters and was now on safe and secure ground. They saluted me for my efforts and welcomed me into their Council.

During this year I received transmissions of short stories from my Pleiadian friends. My guides said it was important that I focus on writing and sharing them because they were training me to be their scribe. I added some of the stories to my astrological lessons and created a book of short stories titled A Treasure Trove of Gems. I loved the stories because they reminded me of my childhood when my father told spontaneously made-up stories to my little sister and I before we went to sleep at night. He would not complete the stories and we would pester him to finish them the next time he was home. He wasn't often there at night but when he was he would tell us a story. I felt story telling was a great gift her gave us.

In meditation later in July Uriel and Gabriel took me into space again saying we were waiting for a Sirian star ship. When it arrived I became very excited, eagerly went on board and spontaneously hugged the four guys in the 'cockpit'. I felt completely safe, as if I belonged there. I felt I'd come home. Following this warm greeting we moved under the sound wave tunnel to meet again Athenia, my star sister. She was the one I'd been introduced to recently, through the universal greeting. She said I would be returning to Sirius following completion of my Earth walk.

When I returned to my 3D world and wrote her words in my diary I felt the 'rightness' of them. Athenia and I had such a strong soul connection that I felt I knew her on a very deep level. Maybe we were from the same soul family, or soul group?

Writing these notes in my manuscript brings to mind a few experiences I had as a young adult when looking into a mirror. Sometimes, when relaxed, I saw a reflection of an extra-terrestrial being with large almond shaped eyes and prominent cheekbones. The image didn't frighten, just made me wonder. I didn't tell anyone about it.

The Seven Sisters

Some days later Uriel and Gabriel took me into deep space a long, long way up. To view clearly I had to maintain intense focus. We travelled to the Seven Sisters, the Pleiadian constellation where an orange/blue colour planet appeared in my vision. The orange colour was bright and clear like the colour of a poppy with the blue similar to that of an iris. The three little humpty-dumpty Pleiadians greeted us warmly and took us to an elegant and round marble-like temple high on a hill. Within the centre of this temple, on the top of a beautiful white marble pedestal, was a model of planet Earth. It had incredible light beaming all over and around it. Light beings sat on marble-like benches placed around the model of Mother Earth beaming their love and light to her. They were relaxed, meditative and totally immersed in their work.

We were asked to sit on the benches and do the same, as it was much needed. Afterwards we were invited to go beyond the temple to view an open shaft where bright light energy was collected from Alycone, the central star of this system. This energy glowed and shimmered. It seemed to flow like lava from the top of the open tunnel close to the temple, where a reflector caught it. This reflector caused the light energy to travel up the 'metal' and then beam down intense light over the model of Earth.

On re-reading these notes it seems amazing to me that so much love, light and care is being given to Mother Earth and her inhabitants. We are not alone. I feel very blessed to have experienced all I have and am very willing to share in the hope it will help others awaken to other realities and dimensions.

NOTE: *"The history of ET Contact in what is known by Native Americans as "The Bloodless Valley" is ancient"* says Steven M. Greer M.D ". U.F.O and ET researcher Dr. Greer addressed the UN with detailed, documented and researched disclosure information about this subject. His books *Extraterrestrial Contact: The Evidence and Implications; Disclosure: Military and Government Witnesses Reveal the Greatest Secrets in Modern History; Hidden Truth – Forbidden Knowledge; Contact: Countdown to Transformation. – The CSETI Experience 1992 - 2009* provide illuminating reading. For more information about CSETI – the Center for the Study of Extraterrestrial Intelligence: visit www.cseti.org -To learn more about the Disclosure Project: www.disclosureproject.org

My Soul's History

Uluru is the aboriginal name for Ayers Rock, the great monolith situated in the heart of Australia that forms one of the chakra centres of our planet. Our planet, a living organism, also has chakras, or energy centres, distributed over her 'body'. Some of the other Earth chakras are at Glastonbury in UK, Mt Shasta in California USA, and Lake Titicaca in Bolivia, all places I visited to do Earth healing work. I'd been focusing on sending the vibration of love and light to the Uluru energy centre and, in September, when again focused in meditation, I felt and saw the rock move. I then observed inner - Earth light beings emerge from underneath the rock, and was shown how they inter-mingle with us to spread awareness and light. A few days later, during another meditation, I again felt the prompt to visit Uluru where I observed more light beings emerged. My trainers said that I had played a vital role in the opening of the Uluru star gate so the raising of human consciousness could take place.

During another profound meditation I was invited to sit in the centre of a circle of a group of light beings whereupon my soul's history was told. I was apparently one of the first souls to volunteer to incarnate upon Earth from another star system and I have had multitudinous lives on Earth, many more than most. I also spent time in different galaxies but mostly my incarnations were upon Earth. I was told that I've walked a long hard road and this earth incarnation is my last, and that I am not to devalue my knowledge or experiences. My guides said they honour, love and respect me.

The Higher Self

On 28th September the Sirius Council of Nine took me to an outer galaxy. To reach this galaxy I was asked to sit in the centre of their circle. They must have created an energy vortex of light and love because we spun anti-clockwise until the movement was so fast it accelerated us forward, as I imagine a flying saucer moves. We spun to the left, up, up and up, further and further away, then swooped to the right. I was asked to view. I saw absolute blackness. I was asked if I felt afraid. I said, "No, I feel quite comfortable". We accelerated and again I was asked to view. This time there was blinding light and I was given a special helmet to wear so I could view the light without squinting. My guides said there is dark and light in everything and it is how everything is made. I was asked to become aware of this truth and told that I now live mostly in the light. There are varying degrees of light intensity and, as we spiritually evolve, our internal light becomes brighter. It is how it is.

In mid-October 1997 I was taken to the Sirius Council of Nine and asked to send love and light to the countries and situations they would select for me. I agreed to their request, feeling very privileged to serve.

Some days later I had the realization of how each individual has a Higher Self or Over Soul. This concept can be likened to a puppeteer who manages a group of puppets on individual strings. The puppets form a circle. Each puppet represents a unique personality, a one-time composite of fragments of the over-soul in one incarnation. The puppeteer trains all personalities simultaneously even though, in our 3D world, the timing process seems sequential. In each of our lives we learn to embody different qualities and talents. We then pass them on to our other selves via our Higher Self or Over Soul who operates in a different dimension of space and time. The way to connect to our Higher Self is by consciously raising our frequency through regular meditation, the daily self-generation of spiritual love, sincere expressions of gratitude and appreciation, and by following heart-felt uplifting internal prompts. Combining these processes with images of white light descending into our crown and moving over and inside our body also assists in raising our frequency level. I created a meditation C.D. *A Journey into Love* to guide people into developing this beneficial connection.

The Lords of Orion

By this time, September 1997, I was working with Sai Baba and Tara on a reasonably regular basis. Both of these great Light beings are from the eastern spiritual tradition. In that tradition the most sacred word chanted is OM. In the western spiritual tradition it is AUM and its derivation AMEN.

Towards the end of October 1997 my Sirian guides said that they were always with me because my frequency, based on levels of love and light, was now high enough to sustain them within me. I didn't question what they meant by this.

During my early morning meditation on 22nd November I noticed a space ship hovering above me. It seemed to be close and felt inviting so I entered it via a beam of light and was warmly welcomed by my three tiny Pleiadian friends. The vehicle accelerated. I questioned as to where they were taking me and was told we were traveling to Orion. The three stars in the belt of Orion came into view and the space ship seemed to be aimed at the central star which became brighter and brighter as we approached. The Pleiadians said they were taking me to attend an important council meeting between the Dark and the Light Lords of Orion.

When we arrived the beings were standing in an oval horseshoe shaped formation. There were two beings at the head of the horseshoe, one dark with bright light emanating from his forehead and one was all light. I was asked, by a voice that sounded like an amplified echo coming from all around the space, rather than from the two Lords, if I would undertake a mission on their behalf. I asked them if it was for the highest good of all and according to the Divine Creator's plan and was told, "Yes". I asked to confer with my Higher Self and they said it was up to me. When they were communicating there was no emotion or attachment in their manner. I said that I needed to know what the mission was before I would agree to undertake it. They asked if I would co-create a book with the Pleiadians, about the roles they, and the Orion beings, played in the history of planet Earth. I said "Yes" however I'd also promised the Arcturians I would write their book and intended to honour this promise first. This seemed to be satisfactory so then we left to return to the Earth plane.

A few days later the Council of Nine said I was now an ascended master working on the Earth plane and am one of the few light bearers who 'walk their talk'. I felt deeply honoured by their words.

1998 - A Precious Accolade

On February 23rd the Sirius Council of Nine invited me to sit in the centre of their circle so they could tone me. I shut my inner eyes and could feel vibrations of pure sound echo around my head. My head felt like a hollow chamber, growing larger and larger, expanding out as it was being filled with light energy. It felt wonderful.

Two days following the March Equinox, and during a meditation, Uriel and Gabriel took me into deep space, a long, long way up where I was asked to look around. I saw a great deal of dark, seemingly empty, nothingness but then observed masses of stars. As I tuned in with my inner eyes I saw a silvery and mystical planet that looked like a luminous Moon, and, as I watched, it became a beautiful clear and soft vibrant purple. We landed on it and floated through a wide channel of a liquid silver substance that felt like gentle velvety waves. The substance became a soft pink and felt relaxing and nurturing.

I was asked to view further and saw an amazing light building, very tall and shaped like a pure crystal cluster. It emanated energy waves that shimmered with light. We entered this building, went to the top floor and again I was asked to view. I noticed a bevy of light beings surrounding us, four to five deep. We were in the centre.

I was asked to focus directly in front of me and there I saw Lord Sananda (Jesus) smiling lovingly and directly at me. I instantly prostrated at his feet. However, he urged me to rise and face him as an equal. I found this extremely difficult but eventually achieved it. He asked me to look into his eyes and there I saw tremendous love, compassion and respect. Holding my gaze he offered me an entwined circle of white roses. He said that the circle represented divinity and the circle of life, and the white roses symbolised the purity of his love for me. I accepted his precious gift with humility.

Jesus went on to say that I had experienced another initiation into spiritual mastery and was to be congratulated on my dedication and commitment to this path. He said he was always there for me and that he honoured and supported my work. I felt overwhelmed, loving, accepting and deserving all jumbled into one. He said the beings were the spiritual Hierarchy from 8D and had gathered to honour me, and my progress. Lord Sananda invited me to return whenever I needed to, and to call upon him if needed. He assured me he would be there for me.

Book Launch

Melody, a world famous author on crystals and their metaphysical qualities, launched my book *Gaia, Our Precious Planet,* at an international festival in Brisbane, the capital city of Queensland, in April 1998. She had been invited to come to Australia from USA to give a presentation at the festival, and, because my husband and I had befriended her some years previously, we invited her to stay in our home. The launch was very successful and I signed so many books that my hands became stiff.

It was during a subsequent workshop facilitated by her that I experienced a past life connected to my fear of making a mistake with my astrology calculations. Melody used a particular phantom crystal to enable the students to access their past and it worked remarkably well. My experience was of having been an astrologer in Tibet, based in the capital Lhasa. I had trained an apprentice and allowed him to provide the detailed calculations necessary to advise the most auspicious date to start a war. I failed to check his work and the result was disastrous.

From my high perch in the palace I viewed thousands of dead, blackened and charred bodies returning on wagons to the main street of Lhasa and took into my soul the huge responsibility of this devastating loss of life. The issue came up again this life when I sat for my first astrology exam. I was so terrified of making a mistake in my calculations that my body became paralysed and I had to be helped out of the room. I have also carried huge burdens of responsibility towards others most of this life. Now I understood why and have forgiven myself. It was extreme arrogance and lack of attention to detail that created the original problem. This experience demonstrates the value of past life recollections. It is not the story that matters, rather the psychological soul imprint that perpetuates through each life until conscious of it. Only then have we the free will to balance the karmic scales. Sincere and heart-felt forgiveness is the key to resolution once we understand, learn from and accept responsibility for, the karmic issue.

Australian Walk-About

On 18th May 1998 a dear friend of mine, Karin, invited me to go 'walkabout' with her into the heart of Australia, driving through northern Queensland and the Northern Territory. She felt it tremendously important that another of my self-published books *Tara, Emissary of Light,* set in the heart of Australia, be distributed freely to as many aboriginal settlements as we could visit. She said the book touched her heart so deeply that she was going to go anyway, whatever I decided. She had even bought a new Jeep and car refrigerator so she could travel in comfort.

I agreed to go with her, even though I felt fearful when she initially invited me. I recognized the fear as being an ancient karmic imprint that I would be given the opportunity to dissipate. All I had to do was trust my inner guidance.

We had a fantastic time and visited ten different settlements where alcohol was forbidden. This was a major achievement. Australian aborigines suffer greatly from the effects of alcohol and, when there are no alcohol restrictions, can become aggressive, destructive and abusive. I simply tuned in and listened to my inner guidance and we avoided these areas.

However, I had one slip-up whereby I allowed fear to rule rather than trust. Karin wanted to drive on further to another aboriginal settlement even though it was late in the afternoon and getting dark. I was afraid to risk it.

Instead of driving on we stayed at Hells Kitchen, a remote, dry and desolate outpost on the Gulf of Carpentaria at the top end of Australia. It was aptly named. During the night I needed to go outside to the toilet. I used my torch but slipped on the cabin steps and fell heavily, spraining my ankle badly.

At breakfast the next morning we learned that the aboriginal elders from the nearby community we intended to visit came to the small store regularly. All I had to do was to ask the proprietor to give them some of my books and then we could drive on to our next destination. However, this required me telling the truth of why we were there and what we were doing. It took me until eleven o'clock in the morning to do so. And of course it was easy once I faced my fear of ridicule and rejection.

This entire adventure in trust was a magical twenty-eight day journey, from one Full Moon to the next. It wasn't planned this way – it just happened. Since then I've become aware of how the monthly Moon cycle plays out in most of my adventures. We gave away hundreds of books, and T-shirts with the book cover image on them, and met some amazing people.

Towards the end of the journey we camped at Uluru, the sacred heart of Australia, and were so cold that we chose not to stay the five nights planned. Instead we drove another two hundred and fifty kilometres further into the desert to visit an aboriginal art gallery. The only road was badly corrugated and very dusty. About fifteen minutes before we were due to arrive at the remote gallery I became extremely agitated. An impression entered my mind that wouldn't go away.

On some level of my being I knew we were driving to a place where a special form of healing, using medicine sticks, took place. When we entered the gallery my friend excitedly explored the huge piles of aboriginal art works while I looked for healing sticks. There were none. I asked Tara the gallery director, a beautiful young woman from Melbourne, if she had heard about the healing sticks. She hadn't but asked the question of the senior artist who had just entered the room to collect his pay cheque. He walked very slowly with a stick because he was an old man, in his mid-nineties. He didn't speak very often.

He turned to look at me, reading my energy field through his old glazed eyes. He must have decided I was genuine because, when he sat down, he began to tell a story, faltering at first. As he did so two female aboriginal spiritual elders entered the room and sat on the bench beside me.

The old man told the story of how there had been a tribe of aboriginals living in this area who were healers and they used special "medicine" sticks to facilitate their healing work. However, maybe thirty years ago, they moved to a much more remote northern area to preserve their spirituality, healing practices and way of life.

The old man picked a pair of clap sticks from the collection and offered them to me. He told me that they were not healing sticks but would be my reminder of the time I spent with him.

After this interchange he collected his pay cheque and left the building, followed by the two female elders. Tara had listened to his story with amazement because, in the three to four years she had been art director there, she had never heard the old man tell a story, nor had she ever encountered three aboriginal spiritual elders in the same place at the same time. She seemed bewildered, and asked me who I was.

My friend Karin was happy with her art purchases and I was happy because I had trusted my inner knowing, followed it through and discovered it was accurate.

On the drive home to South-east Queensland we passed through a small town named Tara, so again I had 'Tara's' appearing in my life.

Story of the White Buffalo

During my meditation on 15th June Archangels Uriel and Gabriel took me again to Alycone, the central star of the Pleiadian system. I felt so happy to greet the archangels again because it seemed to have been a long time since our last encounter. To manoeuvre this flight path we hovered vertically and then sped off at a forty-five degree angle. We entered the marble temple, sat on a bench and I sent love through my heart, and light from my third eye, to Gaia. Then a bright ball of light appeared in my left peripheral vision. It grew in size becoming larger and larger, formed an ellipse and began communicating with me. It said it was the spokesperson for a group consciousness that wanted to make contact and would come again when my frequency was higher. It was ready to tell its story. I felt very comfortable with the presence. I then sent more love and light to Gaia before we departed to return to 3D.

In early August I was asked by the Sirius Group of Nine to enter their circle, sit in the centre and listen to a story.

"Once upon a time, in the beginning when only a few creatures roamed the Earth, the White Buffalo and his herds descended to the Earth plane to assist in maintaining balance, harmony and unity to all. Their role was that of caretakers to the land and their task was to maintain group harmony. Their role was similar to that of the Australian aboriginals in the human kingdom.

Many millennia passed and all lived in harmony and peace. The greater good of the group was always the criteria for any action. After some considerable geological time some individual members of the herds chose to ignore the dictates of the group. They rebelled and went off on their own. This was the beginning of the loss of unity within the buffalo herds. The Australian aboriginals have also played this same role in their long life span on Earth. Their unity and group harmony is now at risk of total destruction.

The Age of Aquarius will address this human situation on Earth and White Buffalo will show the way."

I then had visions of the Earth changes needed in order for communities to re-structure and become more connected, as always happens after a great calamity. The Council of Nine said I am an instrument to help bring back group harmony and unity to people on Earth and that White Buffalo woman would help me. I then remembered a very clear vision experienced many, many years ago, when White Buffalo Calf Woman came to me in a dream like vision. This was before I had consciously embarked upon my spiritual journey.

Years later one of my astrology students gave me a Franklin Mint plate depicting the exact vision I had received. I cherish this plate. It shows a peacefully meditating grey-haired North American Indian woman, with feathers in her long hair and symbolic jewellery around her neck. She is reverently holding in her hands the image of Earth from space, and, with eyes closed, sending healing energy to it. Situated below the earth is a pure white buffalo. Stars are depicted above and around planet Earth.

A Re-arrangement of my Molecules

During my morning meditation on the 10th August I felt incredible light filling and expanding my inner spaces and energy field and, as it did so, a subtle change taking place. I felt bliss. I was told that a re-arrangement of my molecules had taken place.

As mentioned previously I immediately forget these

experiences once the meditation ends. It's as if I easily travel into different dimensions, experience consciously whatever is needed for my training, absorb it on some level, write it in my journal and then no longer think about it. However, the experiences and training filter into my subconscious because I am becoming lighter. My body is a wonderful indicator as to where I am 'at' in my consciousness level because I am not able to eat heavy dead foods any more. They slow up my digestive system and lower my vibration. And I feel nauseous when eating them. Sometimes I receive clear guidance as to what foods to completely let go of.

A few years ago I received the message to stop drinking coffee. "Oh no" I thought. I didn't like this directive at all. I usually only had one cup a day and it was black and strong. I loved hanging out in coffee shops with my friends, smelling the coffee aroma but there was to be no more coffee for me, ever. Apparently it acted as poison in my body and affected adversely my nervous system. I stopped drinking it the instant I was directed to do so. I chose to drink herbal and weak light green tea from then on. I still love to smell the coffee aroma.

The Sirian Temple of Light

I was again reminded, on 12th October, that the Group of Nine are from Sirius and part of my soul group before I pioneered the earth plane. I am Sirian and am to return to that plane of existence at the completion of this life. I was also told that, in other lives, I spent time on Orion and collected some of their characteristics. I understand one of these characteristics is my ability to catalyse others into spiritual growth. People seem to know, on a soul level, that when they work with me they will experience transformational change. Some are wary of it. I don't know how I do this – it just happens.

I was also advised that the vibration of the name 'Ashtara', given to me in 1995 by the Elohim, and who want me to adopt it formally, brings light to others. I was then shown how the natal chart is a hologram and can be viewed as such. I have used it in this way ever since. From it I can read the past life themes and issues that the individual has incarnated to resolve this time around, their present level of development and their potential for the future. Thoughts and emotions are energy in motion. The natal chart is a model of the energy of an individual and shows where psychological energy blockages or 'short circuits' occur. When a transiting planet activates the chart's stress pattern problems arise. 'Sparks' fly and the disconnection blockage activates. I do what I can to be a spiritual electrician.

Later in October 1998, during meditation, I was invited by the Sirian Council to sit in the actual circle, not in the centre as I had previously been asked to do. This was an unexpected turn of events. Once seated, they said that I am a part of their group and their only earthly emissary and I chose to play this earthly role a long, long time ago. This information somehow felt comfortable and right because my heart felt warm and light as I was taking it in.

In meditation the following month I was 'beamed' light by Ra, one of the Sirian beings, and was asked by the Council to be their scribe. I agreed. They said that they work directly under the Elohim and I am their only scribe. They impressed this upon me. Again, at a Council meeting on December 14th, I was beamed brilliant light by Ra. I could feel my heart lifting, moving and heaving inside creating a great deal of warmth as the energy transference took place.

This, I was told, was the final step in an initiation process. I had moved through another initiation to a higher frequency of light and was offered congratulations. I was also told that I know a lot about cosmic law and have the gift of explaining complex concepts very simply and would be using this gift on many occasions.

Then on 19th December Archangel Michael asked if I would be willing to speak on behalf of the archangels who work directly under the auspices of the Supreme Creator. I agreed. He said I would be trained for this role and I that I always needed to listen to my soul, accessible through my heart chakra.

On 21st December, the summer Solstice, my morning meditation guidance was to do a process to heal my inner child. So I imagined taking her into my heart and pouring love into her. My heart felt so warm and filled with love juice at the completion of the process and I expressed gratitude to the Prime Creator for the abundance and beauty on Mother Earth. I then commanded that only spiritual guides from the highest dimensions of Love and Light in the Christ consciousness guide and train me. I thanked any guides from the lower dimensions for their efforts saying that I no longer needed their support.

Then the Sirian Council asked me to join them in their circle. I sat opposite the very tall, slim spokesperson Omega, and Ra sat on his left. Omega emphasized three times how I am a part of the Group of Nine and how I make up the nine. He explained we are a soul group and as a group have unfinished business to attend to. I am to integrate the fact that they are my soul group and I am their only earthly representative. As he spoke my right arm began to shake and I felt my spiritual heart expand. Omega's voice was very loving yet commanding and he said that the other members' names and identities would be revealed as soon as I was ready to integrate the information.

That day my serious training with the Sirian Council of Light began.

PART FOUR

1999 - A PRIESTESS OF ISIS

Light Beings Revealed

I was now able to clearly identify some of the individual members of the Sirian Council. The first two are Omega and Ra, previously mentioned. These two enormously tall light beings apparently have been present, in their etheric form, at all my astrology classes. I couldn't see them but clairvoyant students could. They act as observers, and holders of frequency. Omega, the spokesperson, is very tall, slim, silvery and shimmering. Ra radiates so much golden light it is almost too much to encounter. It's as if his heart is a brilliant sun emanating endless light beams of pulsating, vibrating love light. My designated place in the Council meetings is in the circle directly opposite Omega.

Tara, in all her feminine beauty, sits to the right of Omega and next to her is Sathya Sai Baba. These two illumined beings represent the Eastern spiritual tradition I apparently embraced and followed in previous incarnations.

I was having great difficulty in identifying the next Council member. In my attempts I was always asked to start with Tara, greet Sai Baba and then focus on the one seated next to him. On this special day, January 4th 1999, I purposefully relaxed, gathered confidence and focused my inner eyes. I knew I would unveil the light being when I was ready to see and integrate the experience. So I relaxed even more.

It was then Lord Sananda/Jesus revealed himself as one of the Council members. My legs immediately weakened and wobbled, however he looked me straight in the eyes to hold my gaze. He told me I had been at the crucifixion with him and 'know' him well. As soon as he said this I felt my heart pounding and my legs wobble even more. My body and soul recognized the truth but my mind had great difficulty in absorbing the information.

Omega said that I needed to develop a great deal more confidence and acceptance of who I am. As he was speaking I noticed he had long thin dangling arms and large oversized hands. On this day he wore a headdress of a bird, resembling the one worn in a pictograph of the Egyptian god Horus. Years later I read that Isis and Horus, of the Egyptian pantheon of gods and goddesses, came from Sirius.

During my next January meditation journey to Sirius Omega told me how important it was to pay attention because there were major changes to occur on Earth and I needed to regularly fill myself with volumes of love and light, and to feel this energy build up in my heart. He said I would be called upon to go public in the future, from the most unexpected of places, and asked me to do so, remembering that the Council were with me. Always.

On 7th February I was asked to stand before each Council member as an equal even though there is still one member unknown to me. I managed to do this reasonably well. I perceived Tara as a beautiful, soft rounded female with smooth olive skin. Her third eye, a chakra point between the eyebrows, had a dab of ash on it. She wore bangles on her arms and jewellery around her neck. Sathya Sai Baba, in his orange robe with his face framed by thick frizzy black hair, was very mischievous and Jesus/Sananda compassionate and loving. Jesus reiterated that I was with him at the crucifixion and that I "know" him well. When he said this I again went weak in my knees and legs. Peter Deunov, my Paneurythmy dancing partner, was next. I realized that these two ascended Masters represented western spirituality. Next was Athenia, my Sirian star sister, who exuded divine love and purity. I perceived her as light transparent blue, slight yet with a presence of loving feminine power. The next star being emanated a golden glow but I couldn't identify him. He was a strange mixture of a cow's head and body yet had compassionate and loving human eyes. I felt him to embody the characteristics of the zodiacal sign Taurus. I noticed that his four thin and spindly legs and black hooves were often 'tap dancing'.

Ra radiated shimmering gold love rays and Omega, a commanding presence, emanated silver rays. Their rays were often so bright their physical forms were difficult to see.

A few days later, while deep in meditation and sending light and love to Gaia through a red triangle, my guides came through asking that I use the focused light as a strong fire hose. They said that the light was to be used as a cleansing agent and would have a huge impact wherever it was directed. With determination, focus and intent I directed it all around the globe and then had it enter Earth. I aimed the 'fire hose' beam to the Earth's core where I could see it bubble and begin to fill up with energy, like a big balloon. It seemed as if the core was trying to break free from a prison. I maintained focus and noticed how the core pulsated and struggled. Then it subsided. Gaia wasn't quite ready – for what? I didn't know.

During a meditation on 15th February a similar process took place. I called upon my guides to help me focus on sending love and light to Mother Earth and again saw a light beam appear in my third eye chakra. This light passed through a red triangle and circled the earth. I focused it on the centre, as if to pin Earth in place, and a lop-sided and spinning bulbous blob appeared. It seemed as if the light beam wasn't quite piercing its target because it was slightly off-centre. The bulbous blob was pulsating strongly and appeared to have a film over it. The film broke and began to ooze gooey, thick old blood and guts. The split widened and more blood and guts spewed. A placenta intuitively came to mind. The split continued until the whole bag of contents released. All this time I held the light steadfast. When the final outpouring was complete the light beam lifted and I felt a tremendous sense of peace and accomplishment. I knew something profound had transpired. The placenta vanished, leaving no trace.

On my return to 3D I wrote about this experience in my journal and couldn't let it go. I have such a deep and close connection to Gaia, Mother Earth, and feel she is preparing for a major change, a shift of massive proportions. We humans are to experience the shift with her and the more light of higher consciousness and divine love we embody the easier we will experience the shift. I completely trusted my trainers and training knowing they are very real on some dimension. I understand that what occurs in other dimensions has its physical manifestation in 3D. I didn't try to analyse or rationalize my experiences because my intention was always to operate from my heart and be in present time as much as I could, helping as many people along their journeys as possible. I understood I was being given these experiences for a purpose but there was no way I could think, or imagine, what it could be, so didn't try.

I experienced another re-arrangement of my molecules on 17th February during my meditation. This was quite a blissful experience whereby I feel subtle light, or electrical activations, throughout my head and body. The molecule re-arrangements seemed to occur following a powerful and momentous love-based feeling event. Following the molecular re-arrangement Ra appeared and beamed rays of liquid love light into my heart and I felt it go right through my entire torso.

A couple of days later my guides said that I now operate on five, six and seven dimensions, currently hovering between these levels. The 'hovering', I was told, would soon regulate.

On next visiting the Council I was again asked to stand and again greet each member individually, as an equal. As per usual I started with Tara, then Sai Baba and then Sananda (Jesus). They placed their outstretched hands palms up so I could place my palms down upon theirs. So did Peter Deunov my sacred circle-dancing partner. The next being around the circle was Athenia, my Sirian sister. I still couldn't identify the next Sirian although I greeted him in same manner. I've named him 'Cows head and tap dancing shoes'. His eyes are so gentle, compassionate and loving.

Ra's body is so light and radiant it is almost without form. He radiates love via golden light rays. Omega radiates silver light and is a commanding presence. He asked me to rise to become taller, and then shrink back to size. He had me practice so I could do this at will. He told me that this evening I would have the opportunity to jump into the chasm of the unknown. This must have happened during my sleep because I didn't record anything.

A few days later I became involved in another deep Earth meditation invoking my guides to assist. I focused my third eye on a beam of light. This time I concentrated on both the Middle East and Australia. I circled Australia pinpointing Uluru. As I focused the light beam I noticed sparks fly out from the rock and was told the frequency emitted was transmuting dark into light. I was asked to move the beam around the rock clockwise. Then Omega and Ra beamed such intense love and light into my heart that it filled up. I felt my heart glowing and overflowing and the warmth radiated through my entire torso. The experience was very powerful.

I became aware that I was now guiding some of my own meditations rather than waiting for instructions. The guidance came through me as intuition and knowing, rather than direct telepathy.

The Star

Towards the end of February I hosted a seminar conducted by a North American native Indian. It was a powerful experience for everyone present, including me. The facilitator took us on an inner journey into space. During the process I noticed one particular star. This star drew closer and closer and I saw it enter through the roof of the room and hover over my crown. I felt it enter my being where it exploded. I felt myself becoming the star, radiating white light and, at the same time, realized that an energetic fusion had taken place.

A few days later I flew to America to spend time in Denver with an author friend who had arranged a book launch and signing. *Tara, Emissary of Light* was the book and it is an adventure story about an emissary from the star system of Sirius on a mission to planet Earth. Australia, the most ancient of continents, is the destination. The exciting story depicts Tara's journey and the remarkable events that unfold on her first intergalactic peace assignment. Her task is to help bring about a peaceful resolution to diverse problems. However, there are those in powerful positions with vested interests in keeping the people divided.

The launch was extremely successful and two days later I departed for Atlanta, USA, to negotiate with New Leaf Distributors to distribute my five books. The negotiations also proved successful. During this trip I attended an astrology conference specifically to learn more about medical astrology. I had been studying and applying the teachings to myself for years, healing all my ailments however I wanted a few more tips from the experts. My method was to combine metaphysics, spirituality and astrology because I found this combination worked exceptionally well. I believed in it and was disappointed to find this wasn't the academic approach to medical astrology. However I attended as many lectures as possible and integrated what I could, adding to my knowledge 'tool box'.

On my return home I began classes in medical astrology.

Gaia's Heartbeat

I was told, during meditation, that I am now accessing the Sirian Council easily so have no need to do the preliminary deep breathing and relaxing and that it is only when I lower my vibration that I lose contact. The Council spokesperson, Omega, said that I had needed to go overseas on my own to embody a higher vibratory level. He told me that he would always be present at my classes and that the Council's purpose is to raise the consciousness of humans to a higher vibratory level, and, as one of the group, it is my role also.

I was beginning to understand how I live and operate in parallel realities.

A few days later my guides asked me to act upon my uplifting and joyous feelings because this was how they prompt me. I am also to watch out for synchronicities and signs, and act appropriately on what I notice.

During a meditation a few days later I again visited Gaia's core and observed the sheath around the balloon/bubble begin to split. I was told the birth would be a long hard labour and that another Earth was to be born, a new life with a new consciousness.

At the end of May my guides showed how the astrological transits could be used as a calendar to determine when earth changes are to take place. The Moon, they said, is an important protective device because it prevents Earth from being bombarded by excessive cosmic winds. Saturn is always involved in change because, as the archetypal Lord of Time and Karma, he is the 'time-keeper'. I haven't worked with this system as much as I could have done because my focus was on guiding and supporting students and clients develop greater self-understanding and higher consciousness.

During this same meditation I was taken to another mountaintop and asked to view. I saw the Creator's incredibly magnificent playing field and then noticed the rising of our Sun. I was asked to look behind me. I saw the Full Moon reflecting the light of the Sun with the earth out of the way. Earth was spinning on her axis. I then saw earth's backside blot out the light of the Sun from the Moon. It was very graphic. I was then asked to look at the Moon, but couldn't find her because all was dark and black. I knew it was there but couldn't see it. I felt and sensed that if a comet, meteorite, or spacecraft were to come to earth it would be at the time of a New Moon because it would be the most visible. I also realized how vulnerable earth would be if something were to damage our Moon.

With my guides on 2nd June I travelled to Earth's core again. I experience and feel Gaia (Mother Earth) as a feminine archetype so work with her in this way. I also work with the other planets in our solar system in the same manner, as mentioned previously.

On this day I could feel Gaia's heart beat. I placed my heart against hers and poured as much love into her as I could generate. Then I noticed her heart beat becoming irregular. I looked down and saw her bulbous womb bursting, membranes were splitting open and the pulsating embryo showed itself. It was struggling to be born. The contractions were very strong but then subsided. I wiped Gaia's sweaty brow and again placed my heart upon hers. She relaxed and asked me to go because she wasn't yet ready to give birth. She said that it would be soon. I again wiped her brow, then left, feeling a great deal of empathy and compassion for her plight.

A few days later I again travelled to Gaia's core and viewed the 'baby' being born. It was an ethereal substance attached by a silver cord that floated upwards. The cord greatly restricted the substance so I asked Gaia if she would like me to cut the cord. She said, "Yes" and I used a pair of silver scissors. The shape rose to the heavens whereupon I viewed it being embraced by the Divine Creator. I knew it would be safe. Then I turned my attention to Gaia who was exhausted but happy. I cheered her up, bathed her brow and gently placed a blanket of pink roses over her to enable her to rest peacefully. She was at peace. I asked my guides about the significance of this experience and was advised it would be made clear at a later date. My job was to record it.

Abraham's Message

During meditation on 8th June a guide called Abraham came to tell me that it was time to begin my karmic duty. Apparently I had agreed, aeons ago, to be a pioneer in a project for which I have been in training. Now it was time for the work to begin. I was to "tune in" each day to receive instructions. And then on the June solstice I received the relevant transmission.

"It is I, Abraham. I will come to you in the times to come as we have much work to do together. Do not get confused with who I am and what you read. I am from Sirius and a part of the Group of Nine. The Council from Sirius and I are not under Annunaki control. I may have been once but am not now. I have evolved beyond that, as you have also. Together we have work to do. I have not incarnated upon Earth, however I have been in contact with many earthlings

via channelling, as you call the process. I slip into human's minds when their frequencies are high enough to receive me and when their minds are engaged in a dreamlike state.

The crystals you are working with are part of your process at this time, opening you up to be more receptive to Earth energies. This is needed before your real work for the world can begin. It is all to do with energy and building forms according to ancient teachings. The crystals will help you access your memory. We will guide you to the appropriate stores, books and people you need for this work. Trust. It will be simple and fun.

Listen to the guidance from the stones. Tune into them and they will guide you to your function. We respect and admire you for your willingness to go along with our impulses. Always check within your heart to receive confirmation. Whenever there is coldness, deadness or heaviness do not follow those promptings, as it will not be from us. Our collective consciousness is known as Abraham and I am the spokesperson for that consciousness. Salute!"

I feel I need to explain about the Annunaki mentioned in the above transmission, bearing in mind we live in a world of duality. There is always dark and light. In my experience the Annunaki are extra-terrestrial beings seeking the light. They may be the Nefilim gods spoken about in the bible. They consciously operate as the dark forces through mind control, seeking to divide and rule, and are necessary to enable the conscious manifestation of human light. Light cannot be seen unless there is dark. We humans evolve into light by identifying, accepting and transmuting our darkness.

I have learned, through much experience, that the antidote to overcoming deliberately programmed mind control is to utilise free will by always acting upon our most loving, kind, warm, uplifting thoughts and emotions and allowing them to guide our living.

Part of the antidote is to develop awareness and understanding of, and then release forever, negative and dark emotions and thoughts such as greed, control, jealousy, arrogance and fear. This process requires developing a dedicated 'witness' perspective to one's interior urges. When self-aware, positive action needs to be taken to continually demonstrate a new light and love filled way of being.

If this is not done regularly, until it becomes an ingrained habit, perpetuation of negativity will continue. Such perpetuation of negativity can be likened to a time bomb. Through its poisonous infection untold damage to self and others takes place. The tools are available to move through and beyond the subtle, manipulative power and control games so prevalent upon our planet. One such tool is the study and application of spiritual astrology to one's life.

It's up to each individual to care enough about themselves, their families and the planet to take assertive action to overcome the problem. Why do you think the valuable ancient science of astrology was relegated to the scrap heap during the past two thousand years? Because it enables individuals to become self-empowered and self-realized and those controlling our minds do not want this to happen.

Our 3D blinkers also need to be removed in order to see the truth of the manipulation that forms a major part of external life. This wall of negativity must be broken through before access to higher dimensional realms and subsequent greater love, can take place. Some areas of life where deliberate mind control takes place, through the underlying agenda of power, greed and control, are via the media, education, government, medicine, religion and big corporations.

Wherever there is light there is always dark. This is the duality of our 3D realm. At this point in our human evolution, where a mass acceleration into higher consciousness (light) is taking place, the darkness, in desperation, will do its best to smother the light.

I repeat the last paragraph in the transmission again because it is so valuable:

"Always check within your heart to receive confirmation (of any proposed action). Whenever there is coldness, deadness or heaviness do not follow those promptings, as it will not be from us (i.e. from the base of love)".

I wrote the first draft of this book in Bolivia, beside beautiful Lake Titicaca, and, a few hours after its completion, I received a debilitating dose of psychic poison. This was the consequence of me lowering my vibration while researching the Annunaki and their dark acts. I judged them as bad rather than rising above my negative reaction to view a higher truth. This negativity instantly lowered my vibration, weakened my energy field and enabled a psychic attack. I suddenly become so ill I could barely walk. After writhing on my bed in pain and turmoil for four days, fighting an inner battle between the light and dark, I made the decision to leave the land I loved so much. It seemed obvious to me that the dark did not want this book published. Following this decision I received extraordinary physical and celestial support.

It was as if a red carpet was rolled out in front of me, on all dimensional planes. The considerate Lodge Manager drove me to the bus that took me to the capital, La Paz, and my dear friend and former Bolivian tour guide, Rosse Mary, arranged five-star accommodation at a ridiculously low price while I waited for a flight out of the country. She convinced the airlines to change my non-changeable tickets and arranged for me to catch the only flight from La Paz to Lima that was available that month. It happened to be on a Full Moon –five days after my arrival in La Paz.

This experience was a potent reminder of how my thoughts and emotions create my reality. It is the same for each one of us. Whatever we sow, we reap. The lighter and more conscious we become the quicker the Universal Law of Karma takes effect. We attract whatever we think and feel. It took me months to clean the psychic poison and debilitating weakness from my body. It was only when I re-connected to the Universal Law of Forgiveness, and practiced it sincerely, lovingly and with reverence, that the final healing took place.

Mary Magdalen

During meditation towards the end of June 1999 I was taken on a journey through inner Earth to a pinpoint of light. My vehicle was a laser beam, utilizing a red triangle, and I travelled a long way to reach the light pinpoint. Eventually it opened up into a bright sun ball and I was told that this was creation. There is a Sun and sunlight within every living thing and it is through this Sun that creation forms. I was then asked to merge into this sunlight within the body of Gaia. I felt this could only happen when my own sunlight was as radiant as I could generate so I focused on raising my inner light to a higher level of brightness, and then merged. The dual lights increased the radiation. This then is how light is spread, I was told. When two Sun balls fuse, ignition occurs. I was asked to teach this concept.

I was then taken to the Council of Nine and invited to greet each individual member again, and I could just about do it as an equal. Then I was asked to consider the big picture of my life, with all its different facets, and was told I would never be bored.

So I went above my life and imagined myself as a ball of light. I could then see myself, as that ball of light, linking Australia to Bulgaria, where I travelled in 1996 to learn the sacred circle dance, Paneurythmy, and America, where I travel each year to visit my son and his family. I could see how these places formed a triangle. Then I was given the vision of myself as a point of light linking India with South America. These five points of light formed a pentagram. I was then shown the vision of being a hub of a wheel with all my students around the rim, forming sunbeams. The students go back into their lives and spread their light, and so on.

Before the above experience, and, as I was entering a deep state of meditation, I had the understanding that Earth (Gaia) is like humans, or we are like her. She has darkness in various parts of her body stored in her cellular memory. The darkness acts as a magnet, attracting other darkness to it, hence Bosnia, Kosovo, Vietnam and the Middle East, etc. Old wars were once fought there and that negative energy imprinted into the land attracts more darkness to it. "How does the darkness dissipate?" I asked myself. "The same as with humans," was my instant reply. "It dissipates only through conscious awareness and the willingness to transmute it into light."

I Am An Experiment

I felt it was time to expand my knowledge and wanted to study astrology from a deeper, evolutionary soul perspective so I purchased, from a USA astrologer/teacher/author, a series of videos and books in order to do so - in the comfort of my living room.

One afternoon, following a morning class, I put the first video into the TV. However, a strange thing happened. I couldn't see the male teacher on the screen. Instead I saw a serene and beautiful feminine 'goddess' type woman staring at me. Whoops! What was happening? I thought.

My meditative experiences into other dimensions were one thing but here I was sitting in my lounge chair in the middle of the day with my eyes open, eager to learn. I turned the TV on and off and the same thing happened. My husband could see and hear the male teacher very clearly on the screen, and made derogatory comments about him, but I couldn't.

I couldn't work it out so left it and tried the following day. Again the beautiful goddess appeared on the screen. The same thing happened the next day. I then realized that this beautiful goddess from another dimension wanted to share something with me so I decided to close my eyes and relax into the experience.

What followed changed my life. I was taken into the life of Mary Magdalen and I temporarily became her, and felt all she did at the time. She was a strong, determined and empowered woman, on a mission. Her mission on that day was to meet with her beloved Yeshua, her name for Jesus. The love she had to give and the ecstatic union to be experienced was that of a higher plane involving not only the physical but also the emotional, spiritual and higher mental bodies. She had been well trained for this role in an Egyptian mystery school at a temple dedicated to Isis, the great mother goddess.

She was wearing a long, and quite heavy, reddish brown textured gown to her ankles. These, I noticed, were thick, like Aquarian ankles. She wore strapped leather sandals and was walking along the shores of the Sea of Galilee. She did not like the feeling of the sand between her toes and under her feet. However, nothing was going to stop her from her sacred mission and destiny.

And then I came out of this scene and into my living room. I had obviously been given whatever was needed at the time and it took a lot of integrating. I had experienced many past lives before, during the years of past life regression and re-birthing, but none without my intention and in an awakened state in my own living room. I didn't understand the significance of what I experienced, or its personal and astrological implications, but wrote it in my journal for future reference. It is only now, when writing my final edit, that I wonder what the connection is between evolutionary astrology and Mary Magdalen. I'm sure I'll find out when the time is right.

Intuitive Words

On the 13th September, during meditation, I was again taken to the Sirian Council and asked to greet the council members individually while seated in my place in the circle. Athenia offered to be my healing guide and I accepted. She is a very empowered Virgo type, exceedingly efficient, effective and precise. Even now, in 2012, I hear her telepathic voice speaking the word "precisely" whenever I 'connect the dots' of a life puzzle. It's then I know my realizations are correct.

During a particularly powerful meditation a few days later I felt I was being embraced in the arms of the Supreme Creator. I stayed unified in mind, body and spirit for some time and felt the ecstatic bliss and oneness of this wonderfully expansive experience. It seemed to last for a very long time.

The following day the American Indian teacher challenged me by asking me to reflect upon the birthing of the new Earth, and to express what it means to humanity. I hadn't told anyone about my meditative experience with Gaia but somehow he tuned in, saw it and knew.

What naturally flowed from my mouth without thought was that only those humans who have done their inner healing work to embody greater light and divine love would be able to re-incarnate upon the new Earth. Gaia must cleanse herself of negativity and only those awakened and conscious souls, operating their lives on a higher frequency band of light and love, would be able to manage her new vibration.

Before the birth the waters will break indicating that many huge floods and tidal waves would come. Then the placenta, with all its congealed blood from aeons of horrible wars must also birth, and this may take a war to end all wars.

As I'm writing this final edit the original cover of my book, *"Gaia our Precious Planet",* and its meaning entered my mind. In 1996, when my oldest granddaughter was four and a half years old, she painted a remarkable picture. On a black background she painted three spheres, two green and blue and one bright yellow. She also painted pink trees, hugs and kisses. When I asked her to tell me about her painting she said, "The big ball in the middle is the Earth, the yellow ball at the back is the Sun. The pink drawings are the trees that grow on the Earth and the hugs and kisses are because I love Earth so much". I asked, "What is the smaller ball, Natalie?"

"Grandma, that's the second Earth."

There are many people incarnate today who have memories of the truth of my experiences. Through my sharing of them they will awaken to a truth they know, feel and understand on a subconscious soul level.

A Title Remembered

During my morning meditation on 17th October the Sirian Council again asked me to greet them individually, face to face. The council was intent on me understanding and integrating this process, and it's obviously being repeated until I do. I also feel there is something else for me to realize and integrate.

Again I began with Tara. She invited me to merge with her energy and, when I did, felt incredible love. Sai Baba and I had a most enjoyable fun conversation and Jesus/Sananda asked me to call upon him any time for his wisdom, love and guidance and that he was always with me. Peter Deunov and I danced and Athenia and I embraced. Abraham was the name given to me for 'Cow's head and tap dancing shoes' and this day I placed my third eye to his. Ra transmitted light beams and Omega placed his hand on my heart and I did the same to him. This seems to be a Sirian greeting.

Omega, appearing very serious, asked us to sit. He then told the group that Ashtara is a title that means commander of the angelic forces and, as such, carries a strong flame. This flame would attract many. However, he said, there was still much inner work for me to do and now that I am able to consider myself equal to them the work could continue. I would now be more effective in the work I had chosen to do before incarnation so my 'troops' can begin to gather around me.

I was going to omit the above 'commander' conversation because it seemed pretentious but, as I was about to delete, I recalled an earlier related incident. At that time I had been asked to present the Panuerythmy sacred circle dance at a large Mind/ Body/Spirit festival and was either preparing to dance with my group or had just concluded the dance.

A male friend approached saying he wanted to introduce me to a special friend of his, an entrepreneurial businessman. I willingly agreed and walked with him towards a well- dressed man. I looked lovingly into his eyes and gave him a hug. As I embraced him he suddenly started to sob. I held him more tightly as he sobbed more. And then, when he was able to speak said, "Commander, I am so happy to see you again". At the time his words, relating to his distant soul memory, didn't mean anything to me, until I received the above advice. And then I forgot about it, until now.

Discrimination

On 25th October and during my morning meditation I was again taken to the Council of Nine however this time we were seated at a boardroom table. I was asked to absorb their respective energies, to feel and identify each aspect and quality and to accept they are part of me. I was also asked to understand and integrate the fact that we are one group consciousness broken into nine separate strands, each strand playing a specific role within the whole. They wanted to know if I was willing to write another book for them, that it would be fun, and I would laugh. I agreed. (This could be it!) Then they said I needed to move through a few more psychological barriers, especially beliefs, and am to ingest Sai Baba's ash to help this process.

A couple of days later, when again communing with the Council, I was invited to merge with Tara, Sai Baba, Peter Deunov and Jesus/Sananda. Each one felt as if I was merging with God/Goddess/All That Is. While merged I felt as if all wisdom and knowledge was within me. On separating I felt an individual, cut off from God/Goddess and seeing things differently. I felt saddened yet understanding at the same time.

As I merged I felt each one's individual qualities e.g. Tara's femininity and inner and outer beauty, Sai Baba's humour and playful spirit, Jesus' compassion and love and Peter Deunov's strength and commitment. I stayed merged with him for sometime until I fully integrated his characteristics.

I once read that some people who had a Near Death Experience said they merged with a Divine Presence feeling as if they had all knowledge and wisdom of the Universe within them. Obviously one doesn't need to suffer near death trauma in order to have this blissful and ecstatic 'merging' with Divinity.

I again visited the Council on 12th July and this time was invited to look into the eyes of each member. I felt I melted into each one of them. They asked me to sit and close my inner eyes and allow their toning sounds to waft through me because this would enable my vibration to rise. I did so and felt and heard Tibetan bells and the chanting of AUM as well as other beautiful sacred sounds. After what seemed to be a very short period of time I was told that the frequency raising process was complete. I could feel myself vibrating, like a tuning fork, as a result of their amazing harmonics.

A few days later I was taken in a spacecraft to Orion and we entered the starry gateway through the central star of Orion's belt. Again I was brought before the Orion Council who grouped in a horseshoe formation. Uncomfortable memories arose, as feelings, from deep within me.

As experienced before, the Dark Lords were grouped to one side and the Light Lords on the other. The two Lords at the top of the horseshoe represented the balance between dark and light. These two Lords asked if I was willing to be their emissary. I questioned each of them in turn as to whether the work would be for the greater good of all and was told it would be. I asked if they were from the highest realms of light and love in the Christ Consciousness and was told they were. I questioned as to what the work entailed and they said it would be writing and speaking.

I told them I felt honoured by their invitation but was unable to say, "Yes" at this stage, because of ancient memories. I felt I needed to understand the role of Orion in the greater scheme of things, and my part in it, before I could agree to their request. I suggested they ask me again sometime in the future.

Then I was back on the spaceship and amongst the Sirian Council of Nine who applauded me for being discriminatory, which they advised, was my current lesson. They also told me that I have star consciousness.

Forgiveness

On July 30th I was asked by Sananda/Jesus to buy a copy of The Dead Sea Scrolls and read it. I tried to read it after purchase and struggled because it seemed far to dry to absorb. From memory it's about the life of the Essenes and some of it is to do with the time Jesus was an Essene. I have the book in my library and will read it now (2012) so I can share my findings with you.

I opened the book at random to page 243. The section was number 32 and contained the heading *A Horoscope Written in Code*. It is scroll number 4Q186. These ancient scrolls were found around 1946 by a tribe of Bedouins in the Qumran caves area of Judea, close to the Dead Sea. Scholars identified the remains of 870 scrolls. The translation and interpretation work was painstaking and the first English publication was in 1996. Apparently one of the difficulties encountered in the translation was finding scholars with enough knowledge and time to sort through the huge amount of material. In the fourth cave alone there were an estimated 15,000 fragments. Since 1948, when country boundaries were re-drawn, Qumran has been situated in Jordan and I visited there in 2010, upon an inner directive. My directive was to be in Israel on the 1/1/2010 and follow the exile route of Mary Magdalen. The details of that visit, and the adventures experienced, are written in the sequel to this book, *The Magdalen Codes*.

Translators say that the information in scroll 4Q186 is the closest thing to a scientific treatise that has yet emerged from the caves of Qumran. The text combines astrology and the ancient science of physiognomy in an attempt to determine the character and destiny of individuals. Physiognomy is the study of facial features and each feature describes certain qualities and characteristics of that individual. By the time the scrolls were written this was already an ancient form of divination. Apparently more ancient texts on this subject are known to have come from Mesopotamia. The scroll text uses physiognomy as an adjunct to astrology and describes in detail the light and dark characteristics within each individual, according to their horoscope, and their inherent potential, as does modern astrology. The text also includes numerology. The author of the text believed that Spirit moves through the blood and to all parts of the body.

Significantly, this is a message my Sirian guides gave me – that they are always present with me, in my body. I also realized that this ancient astrology practice was known during the time of Jesus and Mary Magdalen, and is the reason it was so familiar to me. My soul remembered it.

Other chapter headings that attracted me were:

57 – The Phases of the Moon; 82 -God the Creator; 83 – Prayers for Forgiveness; 88 – The Secret of the Way Things Are; 111 - The Words of Archangel Michael and 123 – An Aramaic Horoscope.

I'll return now to my 1998 story. For the past few weeks, while attempting to study advanced evolutionary astrology, I'd been processing a past life involving the people present at the crucifixion of Jesus. Mary Magdalen was there. There was one person in particular I believed had betrayed Jesus and I felt a deep unresolved emotional charge around that experience. It was time for that charge to be identified, embraced, forgiven and released.

I again experienced re-living that period of time. And, from my now higher perspective, was able to see and understand the truth. I consciously and with great feeling and intent cut the aka cords, the psychic threads that bind us to others through our emotional attachments. I released all former judgment and forgave the person. I then forgave myself for making the judgment and for the consequential bitterness and resentment that followed me into many other lifetimes. I filled the empty space in my psyche with love, and felt complete. I could now see how Judas played such an important role in bringing about the transfiguration of Jesus into Christhood and how Jesus had known he would do so.

I was then taken to the Sirian Council to sit in front of Jesus/Sananda. I saw him in a different light. He was strong, handsome, tall and very self-assured. He radiated strength and compassion and also had a twinkle in his eye. I stood tall, straight and equal. I felt I was a Priestess of Isis and his counterpart. Feelings of love welled up in my heart for him. He told me that my very deep and profound forgiveness of Judas would filter through to all of humanity and that the path of history could now be re-written.

He asked how I felt about this and I said it seemed right. I was quite detached, without any ego hooks whatsoever. I was then asked to acknowledge my value.

Ashtara

During a meditation in mid August, in the presence the Sirian Council, I was asked to close my eyes and allow the Group's toning to wash over me. I could feel a vibratory shift in my body as they toned seven 'Aums', one for each chakra. I was again asked to greet each member individually and felt much more confident with Jesus/Sananda, being able to look at him as an equal, eye to eye.

Omega said that my new path could now begin. First there had to be a clearing of old beliefs before the space was created for a new consciousness to enter. He congratulated me on successfully resolving a very old issue, one that would change the course of history. He asked if I would be willing to focus on going within myself each day, to identify my feelings, because I needed to observe the changes to my vibratory rate. This would require commitment and a dedication to the practice. I was asked to focus on this practice as the next step on my path. I agreed, realizing it was a gentle reminder because I had been neglecting my spiritual practices.

On 16th August 1999 the Council said that it was the first day of a new life for me. From now on I was to be known as Ashtara because I had earned the right to carry this name, as I was one with the Light. It was suggested I construct a chart for this auspicious event. (I didn't because, as I mentioned previously, I immediately forget these experiences when back in my every-day world. Best I check it out now, as I'm writing the story. I did and, oh dear, how much it would have helped me to have worked with it then).

Omega went on to say that all was in readiness for the 'Temple of Isis' to be built and that it is to be built by Ashtara. This message came as a shock. What was a 'Temple of Isis'? How and where was I to build it? I wondered. Apparently I had unlocked the doorway in my psyche that stores the knowledge for this creation. Omega said they would leave me now to ponder on this information. They also left me with the word *Namaste;* a Tibetan blessing meaning the Divine in me acknowledges the Divine in you.

(2012: I still don't understand what was meant by the message – I'd better ask. I did – as was told I would find out 'soon'. Patience – patience Ashtara.)

A few days later my guides gave me a book of akashic (soul) records to delve into at any time I choose. It contains my past and my future. I've not taken advantage of their offer and the writing of this book has been a wonderful re-connecting and healing process, and a reminder that I have a lot to catch up on.

On 23rd August 1999 I again attended the Council and was asked to acknowledge each member. As I was doing so I realized that the two members who were at ninety-degree angles to me were the two with whom I had experienced the most difficulty in identifying. In astrological terms a ninety degrees angle in a birth chart indicates a stressful and challenging connection and, when there are two of these angles connecting to the one point, in this case me, they form a geometric triangular pattern known as a T-square.

The Council members were positioned in a semi circle with Omega at the top centre of the empty space, completing the circle. Jesus and Abraham sat at ninety degrees angles to my place in the circle, opposite Omega. The entire shape comprising all members of the Council formed a diamond pattern, or a Grand Square, within the circle. Following my insight there was a long silence.

Then Omega commanded Ashtara to walk towards him and turn to face the group. I did so. Then I was commanded to step back and merge with Omega. As I did I felt myself merging with him, becoming taller and stronger. Then I was asked to step forward again and return to my place. Omega said that I now had more "knowing" inside me.

A square aspect in a birth chart indicates where the most deeply ingrained psycho/spiritual blockages reside. Such angles represent unsolved issues, often accumulated from prior lifetimes that can be interpreted by a conscious and intuitive professional astrologer. Once the issues are identified, accepted and responsibility taken for them, they can be resolved, through self-acceptance and sincere forgiveness. The effect of resolution is a cleaner and healthier body, mind and spirit, and an emerging higher consciousness based on greater self-understanding, liberation, self-empowerment and love.

A Priestess of Isis

Towards the end of August, Archangels Uriel and Gabriel visited me again. I enjoy their visits because they always take me on space adventures. I'm sure the adventures are purposeful but, at this stage in my evolutionary growth, am not able to work this out. I know it will intuitively come to me when the time is right so I don't think about it. On this adventure they took me deep into space through bands of brilliant different coloured light rays. We entered a small temple whereupon I was asked to sit in the centre. The archangels spread their wings around the outside of the columns and invited me to stand to receive and absorb gold and silver vibrations into my aura. As I did so I felt and heard the beautiful sweet sounds of music. They said their work was done and I would henceforth perceive differently because they had altered my etheric molecular structure to that of a higher vibration. The process felt like an energy bath. I thanked them both profusely, not fully understanding what they meant.

And then on the 4th September I was again taken back into the life of Mary Magdalen. In this life I was married to Yeshua/Jesus. According to the custom of the time children had to be brought up by others in order to learn certain teachings. Sexual relations were limited due to the laws and customs of our Essene beliefs. I had travelled, studied and practiced the Gnostic teachings and had also been trained as a Priestess of Isis in Egypt. It was this esoteric training that enabled my kundalini serpent power to rise through my chakras. On special occasions I wore a gold arm bracelet of a serpent. Yeshua, also trained in Egypt, understood the meaning of this symbol.

I was an independent, forthright individual with an elevated consciousness, well trained in the esoteric sciences. I understood energy currents well. Because of Yeshua's position he adhered to the strict rules of the Essenes. I sometimes enticed him into sacred union and he was conscious of it.

I couldn't be a mother, nor could I be a wife, according to my understanding of the two functions, so I felt there was no choice but to live as the independent female I had trained to be. I wanted to spread Yeshua's teachings of love and did so, mostly to women. At this time not many women were educated, let alone in the esoteric mysteries, and I did my best to enlighten them.

Following the crucifixion I decided to leave Judea and travel, teaching along the way. It was a very dangerous time. I chose Salome as a friend and traveling companion because she was also a renegade from the system. I travelled widely, ending up in France. I did my very best to teach Yeshua's message in foreign lands. Early in our relationship I travelled on foot with him, through much dirt and dust that I didn't like at all. Yeshua regarded me as his equal.

An Ending

When I connected with my Higher Self during meditation on 30th October she seemed somewhat subdued, as if weighed down and sad. I chatted her up, cracked a few jokes and then we went to visit the Sirian Council. There I was addressed reverently and asked to stand beside Omega. This I did and it felt comfortable and appropriate. However, I could see and feel that everyone was solemn and sad, and wondered why.

They told me that, because I was now deemed ready to move on, another would replace them for my regular guidance and training. I experienced a tremendous shock in my body hearing this news, and a deep feeling of loss. My stomach heaved and I felt nauseous, sick and weak.

Apparently the Spiritual Hierarchy had only just advised the Council of their decision to move me on, and this is why my Sirian friends were sad and solemn. Their role as my regular teachers/trainers was almost over. The Sirius Council said I needed to accept they were part of me, and I them, and we could not be separated. They also asked me to adopt the name Ashtara legally, one name only, because it carries a specific vibration. I agreed.

Introduction to Antares

I realized that I was now connected, as one, to my soul/ Higher Self and experience this unity as a loving, strong, efficient feminine energy. On 1st November, during meditation, my Higher Self and lower personality self waited expectantly at my platform/ station. Higher Self displayed a great deal of purpose, responsibility and resolve so I knew something different was to take place. A little later I felt an influx of high frequency energy above my crown and then noticed a spacecraft descend. We climbed aboard. I was invited to look down and saw Earth as a small dot.

I was asked to look up and observed a myriad of stars. One in particular, Antares, seemed to be much brighter than the others. We headed towards it and landed. However, its light was so bright we had to don special protective suits before we could leave the craft and I also had a helmet placed over my head. Higher Self and I strode purposefully to a beautiful domed building appearing to have soft clear colours moving in different colour bands around it. It felt ethereal and incredibly calming.

We entered a light 'room' where there were five beings sitting cross-legged in space way above the 'floor'. They were not quite visible so obviously embodied a great deal of light. I could only make out their faint outlines. I noticed that all around me was gentle vibrating energy. They invited me to sit on an extension stool that I could feel and sense, but not see. When I sat it took me up to their level, a little like sitting in an elevator.

They welcomed me saying they were to be my next group of trainers, if I would accept them. I asked three times whether they were working with the Will of God/Goddess and whether it would be for the highest good of myself, and all of humanity to do so.

They said a firm "Yes" to each question. I felt comfortable with them, and with the Antares frequency, even though the whole experience seemed strange and mystical. I sensed Higher Self sigh with relief when I agreed. They invited me to close my eyes so that each one could give me an energy wash, and, as I did so, felt a distinct energetic transference from each of the five beings. They said their role was to take me further up the evolutionary spiritual ascension ladder, that they were a group of five and I was their sixth member.

They welcomed me explaining they operate on a higher vibratory rate to the Sirians and I was deemed ready to move to this new level. I did much spiritual work while I was sleeping, they said, and they would gradually introduce me to these facets of myself. It was then time to depart so we went back to the spaceship.

When we returned to my platform/station my Higher Self asked to stop for a while and rest. I sensed it had been quite an ordeal for her. She explained it was new territory for her and that we had not reached this realm in any other previous incarnation. I asked if she was Athenia from Sirius and she said, "Yes". She went on to say that the Sirian Council are my combined Higher Self and she is their spokesperson. They are a group consciousness, now expanding to embrace an even higher level, through me. When I grow spiritually and my consciousness level rises, so too does theirs. Everyone is involved in consciousness expansion, each one at our own level yet each still working as a whole within a hologram. After this explanation she calmed down and we descended to 3D.

I made a note in my journal that transiting Pluto in Sagittarius was conjunct the bright star Antares when this experience took place. I realized then how our spiritual guides utilize the planetary transits as cosmic channels to expand human consciousness.

It was Sai Baba's birthday and, during a meditation, I wished him well. He and I still had one-to-one experiences together and, on this occasion, he invited me to travel physically to his home in India. I thanked him for the invitation and accepted. He said he would arrange the best timing and make sure I was well looked after.

Then, as I went deeper into meditation, Higher Self took me into a dark cave. I felt very comfortable, like a trusting and open small child, curious and investigative. Towards the back of the cave I saw a figure of an old aboriginal man who invited me to go to him, so I did. It felt right. He requested that I pass on the information I had hidden inside, from my long distant past as an aboriginal. His words didn't surprise me because I knew I had experienced many past lives in different cultures. However, in this incarnation, I feel a strong and passionate connection to the Australian land. He asked me to open my memory banks at the right time and to do the task well. I agreed, after ascertaining he was from the light.

The "right time" may have been my extraordinary experiences in 2002 when I visited Uluru, the sacred heart of Australia, detailed in the sequel to this book, *The Magdalen Codes*. Or maybe there are other experiences still to come?

Towards the end of November I was again taken to Antares where I merged with the five beings of light. They asked me to take a peace troubadour group around country Queensland because our combined energy was needed to awaken others to feelings of peace. It will also open many doors. This was their first assignment for me. I agreed to their request saying that I needed to take my assignments one step at a time. They also asked me to follow more closely the cycles of the Moon and to feel its movement in my body and mind.

At the time of writing I am still working with the Moon and its cycles and have been doing so for years, writing free fortnightly articles titled Moon Musings. And, for five years, I conducted, and recorded, regular group healing full moon meditations. The C.D.s of these meditations are available through my website. I haven't adhered to the peace request exactly as requested.

On 6th December 1999 Higher Self took me on a flying experience and I enjoyed it immensely. She taught me to fly unaided, using my own wings, and it was fun.

Ascended Master Kuthumi

By this time I had collected a large library of astrology books and was studying most of my spare time. However, I wanted a further stretch so, in mid-1999 began re-reading the Alice Bailey material, in particular Esoteric Astrology. I found it intellectually daunting but I persisted. Sometime this year, during meditation, I was introduced to Lord Kuthumi, a spiritual ascended master and my new training guide. He and I became very close and I felt sure that we had known each other in times past. I perceived him to have the most caring, and loving, clear blue eyes.

PART FIVE

A NEW IDENTITY

The New Millennium

Before Christmas 1999 I'd made plans to stay for a week at a spiritual retreat centre where the programme had been designed especially for healers. Each practitioner had been asked to provide a healing speciality to share and I had chosen to teach the sacred circle dance, Paneurythmy, every morning if required. I was looking forward to time out.

Dressed in my white dancing clothes at 6.30 am on 4th January 2000, the first day of the retreat, I prepared to lead the group down the concrete path to a large grassy area near the creek. It had been raining the night before, and, in my eagerness to start, didn't take this into consideration. I slipped, fell heavily onto my right wrist and experienced excruciating pain. The group gathered around, took me inside and commenced their spiritual healing work. The pain completely dissipated in about half an hour because of the love vibration being poured into me. However, I sensed my right wrist was broken and needed either a serious adjustment or surgery.

I went to my bedroom to rest while waiting for transport to the hospital and there I had the full-blown realization of my current spiritual lesson. I was the only one who could lead the dance, wasn't I? No one else could do it as well as me, could they? Even though I felt tired and weak I had to do it. What arrogance. In the embryo position, rocking on my bed, sobbing from the deep shame I felt, further self-realizations entered my mind and I accepted the truth contained within each one.

I also learned to never, ever again say that I was going away for a 'break'.

Through the realization of this life lesson I became aware it was my masculine side and dominant hand that was now out of action. I needed not to be doing so much, rather just be, and allow my feminine side to relax. Following this realization I committed to legally changing my name to Ashtara, as I had promised my guides I would do. The reason I hadn't done so before was because of a deep-seated fear that I would be ridiculed and rejected by my family. I had to get over that one.

My fear and arrogance had caused a serious fall to enable me to return to a state of humility and grace. The only exercise the surgeon gave me, after he corrected the problem and plastered my wrist, was that of holding my hands and wrists in the prayer position over my heart, as many times a day as I could, even when being driven in the car. I laughed at the cosmic joke, and still do, as it was a very good reminder of humility.

After my wrist had healed, and this happened quickly to the surprise of the surgeon, I applied to the Registrar of Births Deaths and Marriages to change my name legally, by deed poll. One name only: as directed by my guides. A change of identity was apparently needed.

After returning from hospital and settling into my everyday meditational life the Archangels Uriel and

Gabriel again took me on a journey to remote view a comet. It was wobbling and appeared to be adjusting itself to line up with planet Earth. This energy would affect Earth, I was told, and there would be many changes taking place. I was to write this in my journal and observe events taking place. I felt blessed that I was back on track again.

My training with the beings from Antares resumed. They told me that their role was to instruct and that their training would be completely different to that of the Sirians. The Antares beings had the task of maintaining my vibration at a certain level and to prepare me for my future role. Their guidance was as follows: a) Adopt the name of Ashtara because it carries a certain frequency that will be felt by many, and will stir memories for them. b) Keep on writing with my left hand, even my astrology articles. c) Always believe, and totally trust, the messages delivered by them. d) Tune in each day by meditating each morning. Whoops! Another reminder. Item two. I stopped writing with my left hand a couple of years ago because it took longer. So, while on this book writing adventure, I promise myself I will start again, beginning now.

The next day I asked my Higher Self if she had any messages for me, or any experiences for the day. My life would now begin to change, she said, and asked that I become aware of the subtle differences. The vibration of the name Ashtara would attract the differences.

More Antares Training

During meditation on January 17th 2000 I travelled to Antares again. When seated on my training stool the Antares beings told me that I have a particular role to play in the 3D world, and that their role is to prepare, and test me, for it. They know I am ready to meet the challenges otherwise I would not be with them. Following this conversation they blended individually with me and then as a collective. They questioned my awareness of their collective energy and asked me to describe what it felt like.

I replied saying it looked like the shape of a butterfly, vertical in the centre and then winging out into two semi-circles. They congratulated me on this accuracy and tested me again. Each one played with the energy of the butterfly shape, moving out a little way into the wings from the centre. They paused and then moved a little further out. I felt the movement in my body each time and told them, so passed their test. When they individually merged I felt the difference in their energy but then went into doubt, wondering if I would get it right the next time round. They immediately picked up on my doubt and referred me to my previous observation because it had been correct.

A few mornings later Athenia (Higher Self) said we were not travelling to Antares this time, instead we were going on a very special adventure. She was her usual Virgo efficient, precise and dedicated self. We entered a space ship, somewhat like a bubble, where she asked me to go deeper into meditation and, when my vibratory level was high, to open my inner eyes. This I did and observed a black sky with millions of stars all beginning to merge together to form one gigantic radiating star, a Grand Central Sun. Athenia said that very few people get taken to this place so I was very privileged, and must have done something right. Whoever suggested that my Higher Self bring me to this special place had recommended we stay in the bubble ship because the light outside was far too intense. We were only allowed to stay a short time.

Obviously Athenia had been given precise instructions to follow and I didn't ask where they came from. Maybe it was the Spiritual Hierarchy?

I was asked to close my inner eyes again, concentrate inwardly and allow the radiant beams of light from the Grand Central Sun enter my body. I felt bathed in divine love and enveloped by brilliant light and knew I was in a place close to God. Then I was asked to focus on the particular area of my body that needed the most healing energy. I chose my heart and felt the very high frequency enter my heart as a warm gush of love-light. After the allotted time we travelled down to my special 'platform' where we spent time integrating and anchoring the higher energy download.

Then we went to my special crystal cave, a place I choose to go in my meditations when I need grounding and earthing. I sat under a rose quartz stalagmite and visualized mounds of gems positioned around me in all their vibrant colours. The emerald and diamond piles appeared a little shaky but they righted themselves after a short time, due to my relaxed concentration.

Again I was reminded to meditate every day. This was because I was becoming busy in my 3D world and not doing my spiritual practices as devotedly as I had done during the past ten years.

Colour Rays

We travelled again to Antares so I could receive an energy transfusion and training. This time I noticed brilliant fluorescent colours, clear and light. They were mostly pinks and purples and appeared ethereal. The five Antareans hoisted my stool up high, then low, then high again. I was asked to relax, accept an infusion of the coloured rays and to understand that the colours emitted a very fine and high frequency. The Antareans said that 3D X-ray is of very low frequency and the human body is adversely affected by it. They then lowered me so that each could merge into me. They explained that the Sirians were my soul group and had experienced 9D and beyond infusions from the Antareans, but chose to remain in 6D. I was to remain in 3D at this time yet be infused with the higher dimensional frequencies in order to fulfil my potential, and they were the instruments for this process.

Athenia took me to my space platform where I rested and then returned to my inner crystal cave for grounding and integration. I noticed there were masses of zeolite, obsidian and tiger's eye all around me – all grounding stones.

On the morning of January 29th Antares called again and, after donning the necessary suit and helmet, my Higher Self and I travelled there. We entered the training room and, when seated on the stool, I was asked to focus on the domed roof of the building and report what I saw. The roof appeared to be constructed of a transparent membrane or skin. I was then asked to look at my trainers and report on what I observed. I saw them as outlines of smiling faces with one very loving large eye in the centre of their respective foreheads. The love and joy pouring from them was a delight to experience. All five merged with me and then, as one unit, we moved in an anti-clockwise direction, building up speed until it seemed we were like a top, becoming one strand of highly charged energy. Then the spinning ceased, the energy dissipated and they returned to their respective stools. I was again asked to look at them closely and saw beams of soft fluorescent pink and violet, with an occasional beam of gold emanating from their crown. I felt I was experiencing a magnificent light show. I was asked to look at their hands and I observed the same colour currents radiating from them. They then directed their hands towards me and I observed the colour rays cross the space and felt the vibrations entering me. They bowed their heads again and I saw and felt the energy rays change. They told me that I could now 'read' energy, and they were pleased with my progress. I could also see how I had learned to let go of my old control patterns and was happily allowing the process to unfold. From Antares we travelled to my space station/platform and then back to the crystal cave for earthing. Again I had to focus on zeolite, obsidian and tiger's eye

The exercise with the colour rays reminded me of a small book I was given when in Bulgaria, titled Colour Rays. In it Peter Deunov wrote about the process described above, however it didn't mean as much to me then as it does now.

The Dragon

On the last day in January Higher Self said that there was work to do and asked me to allow her to lead. I agreed. She took me to a high point in space and invited me to look up. I saw what appeared to be the image of God/Goddess reaching down and I felt arms hold onto us and take us up into another dimension. I was asked to feel and share the difference between this dimension and 3D.

In the very high dimension I felt lighter, weightless, almost as if I was a no-thing, simply vibrating spirit. I had a vague sense of me as a form but there was nothing specific. God/Goddess said that this experience was the state of ascension. Total trust was involved in the process and there could be no personality control of any kind. I felt in absolute peace, harmony and bliss. I was then asked to be aware of my descent into matter. This felt as if I became denser as I descended, vibrating at a much slower speed. I was to experience the same situation again at a later date, I was told, because it was part of my training.

One early February morning Higher Self told me that there was work to do so I went deeper into meditation and waited patiently, doing my best to release all control of my mind. As I did so along came a dragon. This was a great surprise. I was asked to hop on its back, as it would take me to never-never land. I laughed and felt I was having a joke played on me, wondering if Sai Baba was behind it. Because I trusted completely I mounted the dragon.

I was asked to observe carefully. In the distance I could see an emerald city of light becoming clearer as we approached. It shimmered and radiated bright light, like a mass of perfect clear emerald crystals. As I watched it slowly turned into violet and then pink. We entered this emerald city and were asked to sit in a crystal columned temple beside a small stream. I waited, bathed in light.

"Well, what do we have here?" A gruff loud voice said. I stood up, turned around and faced a stern, large male light being. "Who do you think I am?" he asked. I told him his bark was worse than his bite and that he puts on a front of gruffness but inside he is a softy. He replied that I put up a front of bravery, arrogance and stubbornness but underneath I am loving and soft. So, we summed each other up. "What am I going to do with you?" he asked. "And who are you to do anything with me anyway?" I asked. He told me that he is the king of this castle and could do anything he likes. That shut me up.

He listed my attribute as: ethical spiritual values, leadership skills, discipline, able to create structure, and warrior energy. "OK", he said "We'll adjust your circuit so you can be a leader of groups, doing group healing work. Many can do one-to-one healing work but your role is to pioneer group healing. It's much needed." He fiddled with my energy field and promptly dismissed me. I had to have the last word so said I wouldn't go until we'd had a hug. So we did and he 'melted'. I felt empowered. He called the dragon and off we went.

My Higher Self (I'll use the abbreviation H.S from now on) said: "Well that was something different and unusual for this solar eclipse in Aquarius."

It certainly was.

Ancient Wisdom with a New Look

All my 'out of the box' galactic space travel and inter-dimensional hopping took place during deep meditation so I won't mention meditation any more. During it I was completely relaxed, fully aware of everything that was taking place, both inside my body and mind.

On February 7th I was taken in the domed space ship to Antares again where H.S. told me that all shapes have meaning and all buildings on Antares are domed. I reflected on the shape of the emerald castle we had visited a couple of days before and realized it was quite gothic in design, masculine and erect. The round domes are softer and feminine. The five Antareans blended with me and then said that my wrist and hand would only completely heal when

I fully embraced my name, Ashtara. I observed the name – Ashtara - written in the sky, in very large white lettering and then the Antareans emphasized that my true role could not manifest until I embraced fully this high vibrational name. The group blended with me and said that part of me had accepted Ashtara but my personality self was still stubborn and refused to do so. I asked for a human on Earth to help me overcome this stubborn streak as I felt I needed someone to support me through the total identity change.

Only now, as I'm correcting this final edit, I realize who this person was and how he facilitated the change. It wasn't pleasant at the time so I must have been incredibly stubborn and very resistant to change. That is another story. There's also a lesson here on being careful about what we ask for because we are likely to get it, and not in the form we expect.

Athenia took me to the crystal cave for grounding where I rested with zeolite, obsidian and tiger's eye all over me.

A couple of days later H.S and I had a chat. She said that I have a mission to complete as Ashtara and the sooner I embrace and integrate her fully the sooner the knowledge of the mission would come in. She also said that my inner strength and vitality were directly connected to being true to myself as Ashtara. I asked if astrology would play a part in this future mission and she said, "Yes, ancient wisdom with a new look."

The Cosmic Doors Are Closing

Uriel and Gabriel rocked into my meditative space a few days later to say that there was more remote viewing work to do. Again I was taken to view the comet and noticed it was moving incredibly quickly. It had a fiery tail and seemed determined to fulfil its mission. It appeared to be programmed to by-pass Earth, however I felt it would cause huge winds and turbulent seas. I then observed the tip of the bottom of Africa and South America shaking. I wanted to ask questions but was told that the next instalment would be shown to me 'soon'. 'Soon' can be weeks, months or years as there is no 'time' as we know it in higher dimensional realms.

Two days later Uriel and Gabriel took me again to view the comet. Its speed was now ferocious and it seemed huge from my vantage point. God spoke and said, "The doors are soon closing". I asked what this meant and the reply was: "Only a few are chosen – the eye of the needle". I understood this to mean that only a few will ascend because only a few are willing to do the intense and deeply confronting inner psychological work needed. The impact of the comet seemed to be the 'shut off' point. I was asked to read the book I had recently purchased, Conversations with God: Book Three, as it would make the comet's message clearer. I was also asked to record my dreams, as more information would be given to me through them.

Once again, as with *The Dead Sea Scrolls,* I didn't read the book at the time of recommendation. I'll do so now.

The Comet's Message

According to the book Conversations with God: Book Three written by Neale Donald Walsch, our human race is awakening to the understanding that we are all one. It is time for us to remember how it was to live as highly evolved beings, consciously connected to the God force.

Apparently we lived this way in our long-distant past and are in the process of doing so again. We have always been a part of God and always will be. Our evolutionary journey has taken us away from Oneness and now it is time to return.

We are not natives of this planet and the genetic "stuff" of which we are made was placed upon our planet by Divine plan. Each of us can make a difference by being the love that we are. There are many highly evolved beings in other star systems that did not lose their divine connection and they are helping us regain it.

I recommend you read this valuable book.

Antares Training

The following day my H.S. said there was more training to be done so I donned my space helmet and suit, travelled to Antares, entered the domed building and sat on my stool. The five Antareans merged with me. I noticed the first was a male, the second a female and the third was androgynous. Then there was another male and another female. They wound around me at great speed until we became one beam of light then moved back to their seats and beamed energy to me from their hands. I felt the frequencies enter my body. They formed a joint ball of light that came at me, entering my third eye where I could feel this chakra palpitate. I understood that I was experiencing some form of perturbation and would continue to do so because the light would explode existing density of beliefs carried within my cells, drenching them with information and knowledge.

We returned to the crystal cave where the same crystals were used to ground and anchor me back into 3D.

Arcturus

I had a special surprise during my meditation on the 28th February. We travelled to Arcturus and the craft this time was pink and I could feel its loving frequency permeate my being. The space inside the craft felt Venusian: feminine, peaceful and harmonious. The craft appeared to merge into Arcturus where there were even more beams of clear pink and violet colour rays. I was told that these colour beams were the Rays of Light from Source. The Arcturians invited me to get out of the craft even though the ship appeared to be an energetic part of Arcturus. I alighted and felt the frequency to be slightly stronger than inside the craft. The Arcturians said they had arranged my visit in response to my prayer. (I had prayed to meet them because they transmitted my book *Gaia, Our Precious Planet)*. And, they said, the energy of Arcturus would raise my vibratory level through assimilation of the pink Ray of Love.

On return to my space station H.S. took me again to the crystal cave where she asked me to lie directly under a large pink rose quartz stalagmite. I felt my spiritual heart open, as if it was being stretched, pushing against my ribs to access more space. I felt pain in the area around my physical heart and realized my cells were being bombarded with the pure essence of love and the old dense dark memories and beliefs contained within them would not be happy about releasing their hold.

On 4th March we adventured again to Antares. Before we travelled I felt the anxiety of my Higher Self and suggested we meditate together first. We did so and she calmed down. On arrival at our destination the light seemed almost blinding with magnificent, brilliant colour waves of pink and mauve. The domed building seemed even lighter and more sparkling.

Then I noticed the five Antareans had doubles. They were now ten. The ten formed a circle around me and asked if I wanted to move my stool so I could see each of them, or whether they should move. I sat still and suggested they move. They quizzed me, asking me to tell them about the quality of energy they were emanating. In the beginning I felt they were calm then they appeared agitated and thirdly were dancing lightly, like fairies. They then emanated violence, anger, aggression, and finally love. When I felt their violence, anger and aggression my body became agitated and my stomach heaved in fear. I was asked to absorb their love. I felt this vibrational flow enter my heart and it felt warm and nourishing. They congratulated me and said I was learning to read and feel energy. I was being trained and would be totally equipped to deal with the 'flood gates' when they opened. I don't know what they meant by that comment but feel it could be connected to humanity's future. The return journey was the same as previous times.

In early March I travelled to Antares again, however this time I was invited into another room, higher up in the etheric structure. The room contained myriads of lights in the form of waves and transparent blobs. I relaxed and breathed more deeply and the waves and blobs morphed into beings of light. Masses of light beings had gathered in the 'Court Room' to pay tribute. I was placed in a chair that moved upwards so I was higher than the assembled group. I was above them in their centre. Then I heard a voice speak. This voice appeared to come from above however it resonated all around the room as if it was embracing everyone present. It welcomed me and said how great an honour it was for them to have me there.

I expressed gratitude for the opportunity to be trained

by them and they said they would bestow a blessing on me, somewhat like a baptism. They were going to sprinkle a substance over me that would positively affect my etheric field in a subtle way. I felt myself being lowered as if I was going deep down into a nebulous mass of an unknown soft and pliable substance. I felt completely comfortable and at ease, totally trusting. I was raised up again at the same time experiencing something being sprinkled all over me, a little like oil drops. Then I was raised higher and told that my life would never be the same again because the substance would work on my etheric field first and then move down into my physical body.

After this experience H.S. took me back to the craft, down to the station and into my cave where I noticed masses of zeolite, obsidian, malachite and tiger's eye all around me. She also placed a dab of sandalwood oil on the back of my neck to assist in earthing me.

A few days later I was again taken to Antares and asked to look around. I saw three different rays of colour as red, orange and green. These three beams of light played with my energy, first all together and then individually. I realized that these Rays had a consciousness and were highly evolved entities. Then they merged into me saying I needed these three colours: red for power and confidence: orange for creativity: and green for harmony. They went on to say that I was being prepared for a large Jupiter expansion experience. I then noticed some female beings prostrating in front of an enormous light being and was asked how I felt about it. I replied that it didn't feel appropriate because we are all equal. Then I was invited to join the women in the experience and, as I did so, felt loving energy wash all over my spine, in waves of warmth. This is why people prostrate, I was told, because they receive a gift. My trainers told me that I was being prepared for an exciting and broadening experience that would have far reaching effects. I had the image of transiting Jupiter approaching to conjunct my natal Uranus.

It was interesting reviewing these events in 2012 because I am experiencing exactly the same transit. Jupiter takes approximately twelve years to move around the Sun, and, symbolically, around the birth chart. Transiting Jupiter, two degrees from my natal Uranus, moved retrograde two days before I departed on my 2011 overseas journey to Peru and Bolivia to begin writing this book. It became exactly conjunct a few months after my return home in 2012 when I completed the second edit.

I love how events happen in our lives according to the themes and timing of the cosmic currents. I refer to this process as the cosmic joke. Our personality ego likes to thinks it is in charge however there is a much bigger game we play, usually unconsciously. We can become conscious of it, through self-awareness.

Further Training on Antares

On March 20th I travelled again to Antares because there was apparently still more training to experience. This time, as I sat on my stool, I was asked to look closely at the Antareans. I saw the five Antareans and their doubles, trebles, quadruples on and on as far as my inner eyes could see. Each being had a great number of etheric 'doubles'. I was asked to understand and integrate this energetic system. Each being allowed their 'doubles' to move around separately and then brought them back into the one at the centre. This is when I felt their energy to be the strongest.

My trainers said that when focus and healing is needed I am to call in all my etheric doubles so that the greatest energetic force can be given out to whatever, or whoever needed healing. Each of the doubles blended with me and I could distinguish the subtle energetic differences in my body. I was again congratulated and asked to remember the lesson.

I returned to 3D on the same route as previously and again spent time earthing myself in my imaginary crystal cave. This was apparently necessary because the frequency level of the Antares beings was so high that I might not be able to operate fully in 3D without the grounding process. I understood that the lesson being taught was one of unity. Each of us has doubles, trebles etc. operating in different dimensions of time and space and, as we evolve spiritually and gain higher conscious understanding, we can become aware of, and learn to manage, these aspects of self. We are all one, operating as cells in the great 'body' of God/Goddess/All That Is.

During the final edit of this book a girl friend lent me a book to read titled *The Source Field Investigations* by David Wilcock. I'm pleased I did because it explains how some scientists, in particular Dr Peter Gariaev, discovered that our DNA has an energetic 'duplicate' and, by extension, so too does our body. Wilcock also said how Dr Glen Rein, a biochemist, discovered that our DNA behaves in direct response to our consciousness, and that love generates coherence in our brain waves that directly affects our DNA. It's pleasing to know that modern scientists are proving ancient sacred wisdom teachings. I highly recommend you read David Wilcock's informative book. His website is www.DivineCosmos.com and Dr Peter Gariaev's official website is www.wavegenertic.ru

Celestial Neon Colours

Later in March I travelled again to Antares. The colours this time seemed to be much brighter. There also appeared to be more space and clear light rather than diffused soft pink and purple. I understood this was because my vibration was higher and therefore my perception and inner vision had naturally changed. I saw neon colours, purple, pink and gold, in streams or rays. The 'building' also seemed different. It appeared to have greater space and clearer light. The training room only manifested when I stopped at the right spot and it appeared more solid, made from material that looked like white perspex. It was built on a 'stem' that had a mechanism inside it.

The Antares beings came very close and asked me to close my inner eyes and tell them how I felt when they began to work on my energy field. I felt a touch invade it, and said so, but my curiosity and trust were greater than my fear of invasion. Then they moved closer and closer and eventually merged into me. I felt it. They asked if I had any requests.

"Yes," I said and asked if they would help me fulfil my intention to continually be in a state of love, trust, peace and harmony. They seemed delighted with this request and immediately agreed to it. Then they asked me to close my eyes again while they made adjustments to my energy field. Again they questioned as to what I had felt. I told them that I felt them adjust my throat first, and then my thymus. Then it was my heart, where they spent a long time and I felt many adjustments take place there. Next they moved to my solar plexus. Apparently I passed their test because they told me there was still work to be done before the big event (whatever this was), and then dismissed me. The class was over. My return trip to 3D was much the same as on previous occasions.

In early April H.S. and I again journeyed to Antares and, as we were travelling, she said that soon I would no longer need to wear the space outfit and helmet as my vibratory level would be high enough to handle the refined energy of Antares.

On arrival we went to a large and seemingly important room, higher than anywhere I'd been taken before. I found myself standing in the centre of a horseshoe formation with many other beings standing at the back of the room. In front of me were my five Antares trainers. They moved in a line behind me and then merged into one. I could both sense and feel this. It was as if I had sensing eyes at the back of my head. They then formed a semicircle in front of me and merged into one again. I had the understanding then that we are all one and that each person we meet or interact with is a part of us. I was asked to fully integrate and understand this truth. They then merged into one again and that one merged into me. I felt it as a finer vibration.

I now understand that all the people I create in my life are out-picturings of parts of myself. They show me, just by being themselves, my many and varied aspects.

When I returned to my crystal cave I felt I merged with the rose quartz where it became me and I was it.

Departure of 1D and 2D elementals

On April 1st, April Fools Day, I read parts of Barbara Hand Clow's amazing book, *The Pleiadian Agenda, A New Cosmology for the Age of Light*. This book stirred many memories in the form of feelings and I did a process recommended by her. I meditated and asked all the elementals from 1D and 2D to leave my body, and called upon Archangel Michael to open the space for the beings to leave. Hordes of these beings exited from my solar plexus and throat and I could feel and see them leaving. Then I felt them leaving my head as I did the same process. There appeared to be masses in my heart and I also saw them leaving. I thanked them for the role they had played in my life, sealed the places where they had been with a violet flame and filled the empty spaces with brilliant light.

I worked on other parts of my body in similar fashion and in particular my wrists. The beings that left my damaged wrist thanked me for their holiday. I'm pleased they enjoyed it. I saw all these beings clearly and felt I was even more sensitive than previously. I then felt sparks at my crown chakra, activating my galactic centre. H.S. suggested I earth myself now by working in the garden. She said there was more clearing to be done and that I would be activated to do it at the right time.

My training program changed on April 5th. The Antareans asked me to listen carefully and recognize different sounds with my eyes shut. I heard clapping sounds at first and then the clanging of cymbals. Drums and a Tibetan bell were next. This bell had a very deep resonant tone. The Antareans made a collective sound and I was asked to feel where the sound came from. I felt it was expressed through their throat but actually arose from a deep chamber within their heart chakras. I could feel this strongly. They said that I was beginning to speak through my heart chamber but there was still more work to do, and that I needed to experience so I would understand.

A Jupiter/Uranus Experience

On April 9th 2000 Uriel and Gabriel took me to view the comet again. From above I could see that it would by-pass Earth somewhere around the Antarctic with the southern tip of South America receiving the greatest brunt. It will cause floods and tidal waves because of incredibly strong winds. I was told that waves of 'particulate matter' would bombard the area. Chatting with H.S. following this experience I asked her to tell me what was really going on. What was my path and where was all this training taking me? I'd agreed to do the work for the Sirians, to advance my astrology and go public with Ashtara, and to build a particular kind of temple when the time was right. So where was all this Antares training leading? She said my path was to ascend.

"What exactly does that mean and what is this mission I've incarnated to fulfil?" I asked. She told me that I was 'on track' and all would be revealed, soon. And that I have to take one step at a time otherwise I may feel inadequate and overwhelmed if the purpose was known. I felt disappointed. 'Soon' can be years away. I guess I was being tested with my patience levels – and still am in 2012.

The next day I received another energy lesson from the Antareans. Seated on my stool in the lower room I sensed their presence behind me. They merged, separated, merged and separated many times and I could feel and sense it every time. Then they came to my front, joined together and merged into me. I felt as if I had a strong pillar of a wood inside. As they left I felt the 'wood' retract and then after doing this a few times I felt it stay. It was soft and stable yet strong. Their energy was solid within me. I enjoy these lessons because they are experiential and I learn best this way.

Perturbation into greater Light

In my 3D life I attended a weekend workshop with a remarkable USA facilitator, Bryan de Flores. This was on April 17th. I was excited about attending this workshop because transiting Jupiter was conjunct my natal Uranus. This conjunction can indicate that an opportunity is available for greater spiritual growth and expansion, along with feelings of liberation and freedom. This was certainly the case for me.

During the weekend each attendee received a 'blast' of high frequency energy and a clear channelling from the brilliant facilitator. When it was my turn for the energetic transference I felt a deep process occurring. My heart chakra opened, filling me with feelings of divine love. I also felt and heard a 'popping' of energy on the right side of my crown. It felt like an explosion. The image I received was that of a light bulb shattering.

Perturbation certainly took place. Bryan told me that he saw me in a past life, firstly in Siberia working with the wind energy of movement (Gemini) and then as a galactic exchange student (Sagittarius) on Earth. He also said I had six emotional karmic issues still to clear and didn't elaborate on them. I believed these to be self-trust, self-belief, fear of making a mistake, fear of expressing my truth to those I feel will ridicule me, undervaluing myself and a sixth that was cloudy. I had to eat a great deal more food for lunch that day than I could ever remember doing, and drank litres of water. I was in an incredibly calm and relaxed state and had to go to bed very early on Sunday night.

After lunch the following day, Monday, I felt the need to lie on my bed. From previous experiences I knew that my guides induced this state whenever I was called upon to work in another dimension. I slept. Upon awakening I had the most amazing experience. I could feel and identify the Uranus symbol building up inside me, filling my entire inner space. I experienced travelling into space however there were no stars, only a black void. I felt totally comfortable, detached and 'at home'. Then I saw and felt Jupiter enter my body to expand this experience.

I observed a small bird flying in the sky, totally trusting its instincts, believing in its inherent wisdom as it flew great distances across the skies. It knew it would be safe when it followed its inbuilt radar system, being focused in present time and moving with the currents of energy. I felt I was like that bird, allowing the energy currents to move me.

Farewell to Antares

The next morning, during meditation, I asked my guides from the highest dimensions of love and light for a message. The Sirian Council came and I was overjoyed at being with them again. I'd missed them and felt we had been apart a long time. They congratulated me on moving beyond anything I had ever done before in any other earthly incarnation. I then realized they represent aspects of myself. Jesus is my heart. Again he said to me "I know you". I took this to mean that he knows me as a soul fragment of Mary Magdalen and that we are intimately connected through our hearts. Every time I feel my heart chakra expand, it will be him. 'Cow's head and tap-dancing shoes' represents the unusual parts of myself I do not yet know. Tara is my soft feminine, Sai Baba the mischievous happy 'mother' archetype and joker, and Peter

Deunov represents the dance and movement so necessary in my life. Athenia is the efficient and practical Virgo analyst, healer and discriminator and Ra is my radiance. Omega is my tall masculine Sirian teaching energy. I feel so grateful for being able to see and understand this.

The Council told me they were very proud of my progress and that I had now moved to another consciousness level and that the Antareans would assist me to ascend even higher.

I also realized that the cosmic name given to me, Ashtara, contains the names of two of the Council members: Tara and Ra. Each of these Sirian light beings sits in Council next to spokesperson Omega. Tara is on his right and Ra his left. According to Wikipedia Omega is the 24th and last letter of the Greek alphabet and means "great O". In the New Testament God declares himself to be the "Alpha and the Omega, the beginning and the end; the first and the last. (Revelations 22.13)

The omega symbol can be likened to that of the North Node in astrology. In endeavouring to make sense of this symbolism I could see that the "great O" has the energy of the divine feminine to his right and the divine masculine to his left.

I Am You and You Are Me

In April 2000 I received the documents I needed to complete and send to the Department of Births, Deaths and Marriages in order to change my name legally. I felt a very deep fear stir, so put them aside.

During meditation the next morning I again journeyed to Antares where I was guided to a different room and asked to focus on the domed ceiling. As I did so I sensed and saw the room expand and contract according to my thought. Some light beings formed a pillar within me. They then become blobs in front of me. The 'blobs' became larger, forming human-like beings. They reduced to blobs and again into a pillar, as one. This process was repeated. I was tested on this process, always reporting by telepathic communication on what I was seeing and feeling.

Then a single eye appeared, which blinked. I reported the phenomenon to my trainers. I was then asked to comment on the qualities and characteristics behind the eye. It appeared to me to be very detached and without emotion. It was simply observing, and blinked sometimes. The eye was dark brown and fathomless. This was the All-Seeing Eye, and I felt I was the Eye and the Eye was I. Then I was told my lesson was over, that I had done well and was a good student.

I was very quickly taken to Antares again on May 1st. The five beings merged into one and then merged into me. I was asked to feel this process as they repeated it three times. They seemed insistent that I understand and integrate it. Then I was asked to swivel around on my stool so that my back was to them. They then merged with me from behind. Again I was asked to feel the point of impact. I did this easily, feeling their different vibrations within me.

I know that we are one and they represent the out-picturing of the Antares aspect of myself operating in the 9th dimension and beyond. They told me that their training program would end very soon because I had learnt well. They also said that my evolutionary process is to be further accelerated and I will be introduced to yet another group of trainers when the time was right. I felt sad when they said this, and expressed it. They replied there was little more they could teach me because I understand fully that we are all one. I am part of them and they me, and what more is there?

A Record Keeper

On May 10th the issue of my identity as Ashtara arose again because it was time to make the name change legal. Paralysing fear took hold of my body. On one level it was the fear of ridicule and rejection and yet, on another, there was a greater fear beyond my conscious understanding. Was it a fear that the consequences of my name change could lead to a marriage separation? I wondered. Using motivational self-talk I told myself that I must break through the fear and trust that all would be well. With shaking hands I filled in the official forms and sent them off to be registered.

In early January I had been invited to be a presenter at the inaugural Australia wide Wesak spiritual celebration to be held in Sydney in May 2000. I was asked to offer my astrological view point on the unusual planetary alignment in Taurus (the zodiacal sign attributed to the Buddha) and to teach the expected three hundred people the sacred circle dance, Paneurythmy. Wesak is a worldwide spiritual celebration of the Buddha's wisdom and enlightenment that takes place one Full moon after Easter. Easter celebrates the love and teachings of Jesus and his resurrection and ascension. Together these two annual global spiritual celebrations contribute to bring love and wisdom to Earth.

At this amazing inaugural event, and during a group meditation, I was transported to Uluru (Ayers Rock), the most sacred place in the heart of Australia. There I was guided to enter inside the huge monolith where I was greeted by a very old aboriginal elder carrying a walking stick. He took me through a long tunnel into the bowels of the earth. A door appeared on my left. The elder opened this door, we entered the room and then he closed it. He told me that we were as close to the Uluru crystal as we could get and that this crystal contained all the records of Earth's beginning.

The old man said that I am the record keeper and handed me an old, large and very dusty book containing the records from the beginning of time on Earth. I am to write about it. I asked him to telepathically prompt me when I needed to write, and to guide me by feeding me the information. He agreed. We firmly clasped hands to elbow. The deal was done. He thanked me and I left the sacred space.

Note: In the previously mentioned book *The Source Feld Investigations* by David Wilcock there is a quote on page 321 that speaks about a giant crystal buried deep in the centre of the earth, more than three thousand miles down, that scientists discovered in 1995. And, NASA's Glatzmaier-Roberts model revealed a geometric "crystal" pattern in the earth's core. I also mentioned earlier that crystals contain a consciousness and can be programmed to contain and release information.

I only now realize, as I'm completing this final edit, that the extraordinary experience I had at Uluru two years later, one I will write about in the sequel to this book, is part the old Aboriginal's message. I didn't connect the two at the time of the physical experience.

I also now understand that my ascension process was about the mutation of form into spirit. By spiritualizing my physical body I was able to embody greater light.

South America

The second auspicious 3D event of this year, another life changing one, came a few months later. My husband decided to travel to Brazil in South America to visit gem stone mines and invited me to go with him. I wasn't the slightest bit interested in seeing another mine, gemstones or not. I'd been underground many times and seen so many open cut mines, that I was completely mined out. He asked where I would like to go and, out of my mouth, without knowing or thought, came the words "I'd like to visit the sacred sites of South America". So he arranged everything. He travelled to Brazil first and then I met him in Dallas, USA. From there we flew to Peru. The only message I received from my guides before leaving was that of a vision of a stone alcove, shown during a meditation. I was to visit this alcove when at Machu Picchu, an ancient City of Light and one of the eight wonders of the world. There I would receive information downloads.

On the plane from Dallas to Lima I received a simple message to trust the man at the airport wearing a blue jacket. At the Lima airport, before leaving for Cusco, the ancient spiritual capitol of Peru, my husband engaged in conversation with a well-dressed and well-spoken Peruvian man. They were chatting amicably, however I became aware of time slipping by and didn't want us to miss the plane. As I asked them to consider this I noticed they were exchanging names and I clarified our name. We then scrambled through the crowd to reach the departure gate.

Outside Cusco airport we were greeted by a bevy of hawkers, all wanting our business. My husband went off to find a taxi while I scanned the crowd. And there I saw this beautiful Peruvian young woman with a huge smile and thick black hair blowing lightly against her face. I felt her loving and generous essence and immediately trusted her.

She carried a placard with our last name scrambled but recognizable. I wanted to go with her and when my husband came back with his taxi driver I introduced him to Teresa. He liked her so we placed ourselves in her hands for the next few days. She took us to some hotels to see which we preferred and then booked us in to the one we chose. She brilliantly organized our few days in Cusco and arranged for our transport to and from Machu Picchu. Then she recommended we rest for two hours, to adjust to the high altitude, and drink lots of coca tea. When it was time she would come and introduce us to a tour guide who would take us on a tour of some of the sacred sites around Cusco.

I asked her how she found out our name and she told us that her cousin was at the Lima airport talking to my husband and, after our departure, he called her with the scrambled version of our last name. I realized then that he had worn a navy blue jacket.

The experience I had at the first sacred site we visited was very important, although I didn't realize its value until eight years later. The Peruvian tour leader, who spoke reasonable English, was a capable and friendly young man. There were twelve to fifteen tourists in the group from a variety of English speaking countries. When we approached the first sacred site he became very excited when he saw a group of indigenous Peruvians, dressed in bright traditional clothing, waiting for us. The guide told us that he hadn't seen this kind of group before because they usually lived high in the mountains above five thousand metres. They were known as the Q'ero, an indigenous spiritual race.

The Q'ero had decided, in the early 1500's before the Spanish invaded Peru, to move from lower altitudes to live in the high mountains to preserve their ancient spiritual practices and wisdom. They knew of the imminent arrival of the Spanish, and the darkness that would follow, and didn't want their culture and spiritual way of life contaminated.

Our tour guide was somewhat in awe of this group. When the Q'ero leader approached him saying that he wanted to do a ceremony and needed a member of the tourist group to participate, the guide willingly agreed. Following discussion I was chosen. The Q'ero proceeded to do the ceremony, the content of which completely escapes me, however I do remember they were working on the energy field around my crown and third eye area. They then thanked me for participating and gave me presents - a few items of their hand-made weavings. I felt honoured but placed little relevance or meaning on the event, until, as I said earlier, about eight years later. It was then I had an ah-ha moment, realizing they had been instrumental in activating specific information from my soul's cellular memory.

Sometime during the train trip to the ancient sacred site of Machu Picchu we realized that our time there would be limited. Because the train journey took approximately four hours and the same time to return we would only have two hours, at the most, at the site. I didn't worry because I knew there would be plenty of time to do whatever was needed.

We listened to the tour guide's interesting story and then separated. I went to find the alcove in which to meditate, allowing my body to lead. I totally trusted the process and knew it would be easy. Within five minutes I found myself exactly in the place shown in my vision. I was in the Cave of the Condor. The condor is a giant bird, and, to the local indigenous people, the representation of Great Spirit. The carved rock alcove was situated next to an ancient, and well used, stone offering bench, the offerings being given to Pacchamama, the Spirit of Mother Earth. I felt very comfortable sitting there so relaxed and closed my eyes.

Instantly I was shown how, many aeons ago, I had come to Machu Picchu with my star brothers and sisters, most of whom were scientists, on a mission from Sirius. We were pioneers to planet Earth and had chosen to land our craft at this site. Here we chose to create a home, because of the geography and co-ordinates of the land. Our task was to build a 'City of Light', a sacred esoteric school. My job was to not only design the Light City but also to teach in it once it was established.

The download stopped and the scene changed.

I became aware of lines of tiny Andean women, about four feet high, entering my psychic space from the left. The women were dressed in their predominantly red, woven cultural clothing with wide and heavy skirts and small black bowler hats. They moved closer and then their leader stopped in front of me. She asked, reverently and almost pleadingly, if I would come back to Peru, and in particular to Machu Picchu, next year at the June

Solstice and each year from then on, until the mission was complete. She said that it was important to dance the ancient sacred circle dance, Paneurythmy, at the sacred sites that would be given to me. I was to bring a group each year because the combined love vibration, created through the special dance, was needed to re-open some of the closed energetic portals underneath the site. I would know when this work was done.

I agreed to her request. The tiny women began streaming past me, one behind the other, expressing their heart-felt appreciation, respect and love. Their small hands were placed in prayer position over their hearts and their heads were bowed. Tears were streaming down all our faces. The line of little women seemed never ending. There must have been hundreds, maybe thousands of them.

A while later I became aware of the absolute stillness within the cave, and within me. Not one of the many hundreds of tourists above had walked over or into the cave while I had been sitting there, maybe for half an hour or more. I felt such gratitude and humility for the experience and knew my life had changed forever.

I've seen remnants of this tiny race in my many travels to South America over the past eleven years. They were mostly in Bolivia although I've seen a small number in Peru. They are perfectly formed little women, now about four - five feet high.

Some days later we flew to the land of the Maya in Central America and visited many of the pyramids. The place where I felt most comfortable and 'at home' was Palenque in the Chiapas. There the pyramids were built into the natural land as they are in Peru and I felt the same architectural idea, spirituality and culture connected the two. I looked around at the surrounding hills and knew there are many more pyramids still to be uncovered. I was told that I have work to do there, one day.

During meditation at one of these temples I received a transmission from Abraham of Sirius in the form of a story.

"Once upon a time there was a High Priest who ruled the Mayan people well. He had great knowledge of the stars and also much sacred wisdom. This High Priest carried stellar codes. He knew how cosmic energy patterns worked. He knew sacred geometry and geography. He was sent by the star people to assist with the evolution of humans on Earth.

This great man, Pacal was his name, was honoured and respected by his kin. His lineage was that of a highly evolved being. This man ruled wisely and well, eventually passing on to his earthly son much of his wisdom and understandings. His line continues to this day. His reason for incarnation was to pass on, through his lineage, a stream of knowledge so that humans could evolve to a higher understanding of cosmic wisdom. Pacal was a stranger to the land of the Maya, however he fulfilled his destiny. His earthly descendants contain within their genes much ancient wisdom and knowledge which is being activated at this time through certain encodements.

Those of his lineage will remember. They will begin to feel, and through their feelings the knowledge will arise from their subconscious into their conscious mind. The truth will soon be known and archaeology into ancient sites will assist this process. Humans will soon learn the truth of their heritage. It is time for this ancient knowledge to be accessed. It will not arise from study. It will arise during meditative moments. You are one of the instruments through which this knowledge will surface.

Much has been written. Some of the writings skirt around the truth. Some of the truth is deliberately kept secret. This truth will find its outlet at the appropriate time. So it is and so it was."

Psychic Attack

A few days later we flew to Merida city in Mexico, minus our luggage. It had apparently been lost. Fortunately we both had a spare pair of undies and an extra top in our carry-on bag. We had planned to use Merida as a base to visit the pyramids in the Yucatan peninsula area and intended to be there for five days. We visited a few of the pyramids closer to Merida and, on the morning we were to drive to Chichen Itza, the largest one, I felt nauseous and weak and wondered what was happening. I felt as if dark, horrible ancient energy was stirring in, or had landed on, my solar plexus. The closer we travelled to the pyramid, which looked like an Egyptian pyramid, the more weakened and sick I became. When we walked past the Temple of the Skeletons I felt a number of dark 'ghosts' jump on me and weaken me even more. I became so drained of energy I could barely walk or talk. I realized I was experiencing an unexpected full-blown psychic attack. I couldn't climb the pyramid so I had to sit in the shade of a tree and watch the others do so.

When I experience these attacks not only does my body feel nauseous and weak but my brain also. I can't think, nor can I speak coherently. It's as if something or someone sucks all my vital energy leaving me weak and powerless with seemingly hundreds of cotton wool balls filling my head. All I can do is feel. I realized this experience probably had a past life influence and I didn't like it. When we drove to our next destination I needed to go to the toilet, however, after entering the cubicle I passed out and had to be taken to the mini-hospital. I was given oxygen for five hours until my energy levels returned. It wasn't until years later, when I was taken back to the same pyramid during a meditation, that I understood more about the experience. It is described in the sequel to this book. In hindsight I also realize that I must have lowered my vibration by allowing negative thoughts to take me over. My lower vibration attracted like negativity.

On departing Merida we decided to take charge of the luggage situation and insisted we be allowed to check the baggage room. Our suitcases were there even though we had been told they were not.

Belize City in Guatemala was the next place to visit on May 26th. During a meditation there I was escorted to Antares without helmet or suit. The light was very bright but manageable and the rainbow colours brilliant. In the higher room the five Antareans blended into one, then merged with me. I was advised that I could now refer to myself as being from Antares, Sirius and Arcturus. I questioned the Arcturus bit because they had not merged with me. They said it had happened when I was writing the book *Gaia, Our Precious Planet*.

Later I was taken before the Council of Arcturus where the leader held a sword and had me kneel in front of him while he dubbed my head and shoulders as a welcome into his community.

When I was being transported back to the space ship and down to my 'platform' I was asked if I had any questions. I asked where my 3D work was taking me. The answer: "More group work."

Gestation of The Golden Age

As part of my return trip to Australia I visited the small island of Guam. During my early morning meditation and while waiting at my 'platform', a bus arrived with other passengers on board. This was a different means of transport to any I'd experienced before however I stepped on board and walked to my allotted seat. The bus hurtled through space, travelling to the right, passing much debris. I felt the strong pressure of space. We arrived at an area to view what appeared to be a new world in the making. We observed a large area of deep blue space containing a golden orange ball of light. Everything felt peaceful and there was no noise or movement. I intuited we were viewing a state of gestation, a waiting period and it felt incredibly relaxing.

We were told that what we had seen and felt was the gestation period of the Golden Age. *"As Above: So Below"*. The Golden Age on Earth will happen and it is now in its gestation period. Following our return I was dropped off at my station and asked to record the experience. While doing so I wondered about the other passengers in the bus, and whether they had experienced similar training to mine. Maybe I'll find out one day.

Training by the Spiritual Hierarchy

Upon my return home to Australia, and during my morning meditation, Abraham (Cow's head and tap dancing shoes) came to me. He said I was to experience more spiritual expansion and growth and asked that I act according to the impulses of the expansion period.

As mentioned earlier I was experiencing a Jupiter transit and Jupiter brings opportunities for expansion and spiritual growth. This growth is usually in the form of a psychological, spiritual or physical 3D stretch.

During meditation on June 10th I was taken up to the higher chamber situated in the domed building on Antares. The colours of pink and violet reflected my harmonious state of being. One extremely tall being, shiny and luminous with gold and silver beams running through him, offered to blend and merge with me. He said he was the spokesperson for the Antares group consciousness and that I could call him Uran. I agreed to his offer and we merged. He told me that his energy would act as a key to open more doors in my consciousness and that it was time for this to take place. I likened him to Chiron and I was also experiencing a Chiron transit.

Uran asked me to call upon him whenever I needed a broadening of consciousness. I didn't forget this experience and have called upon him from time to time. Memo: I must remember to do so again.

Archangels Gabriel and Uriel took me to outer space on July 19th, much further than I had ever been before, and asked me to view. I saw no-thing-ness - a translucent black void. The Archangels said that there was no further for me to go because I had ascended. I had united with myself, and all of Creation, and there was nothing more. I didn't fully comprehend this information so couldn't integrate it.

A few days later, during a meditation, I waited at the top of my space station platform, allowing the next part of my journey to unfold. The Spiritual Hierarchy converged around me and invited me into the centre of their circle. They embraced and encircled me with their wings and the experience felt warm, loving and totally wonderful. They reminded me that I am a member of their group and said that they are to be my new teachers/guides through their leader and spokesperson, Kuthumi. I said I didn't like the word 'Hierarchy" as its connotation in our 3D world was of a multi-level pyramidal type business organizational structure. We agreed that I would refer to them as Spiritual C.E.O's. They run the organizational structure of the Universe and work directly under the auspices of the One Creative Source.

A few days later the Spiritual CEO's enfolded me again with their wings saying that Kuthumi would devote much of his time to the next part of my training. They asked if I would create the time each day to participate in the training. I said I would and committed to this path.

Perception

On July 31st, under a New Moon and Solar eclipse in Leo, the Archangels Uriel and Gabriel escorted me to a higher dimension of Jupiter to meet with Master Kuthumi and the Spiritual CEO's. Master Kuthumi showed me how our solar system is a physical manifestation of many of similar solar systems operating in different dimensions. Just as we are the physical manifestation of a soul and spirit in a body and have many other selves operating in different dimensions so too do the planets and the solar systems. I embraced the concept immediately and felt I understood it. The Spiritual Masters are on Jupiter in a higher dimension and we can connect with them by using specific parts of our brain. Master Kuthumi said I learn well and he could see why the Sirius Council of Nine was reluctant to let me go.

I asked Master Kuthumi if he was going to incarnate on the 3D plane and he told me that he already had. I questioned as how to address him and he asked me to call him Kuthumi, without any title. Then he asked if I would show total dedication to my spiritual path by meditating daily. I understood this was necessary to keep my vibration at a high enough level to receive the necessary training, so I agreed. I asked if he was the World Teacher and he said, "No" that was Lord Maitreya, and that he, Kuthumi, was his disciple.

On August 8th the Archangels took me to higher dimensional Jupiter where I was told that I am one of twelve disciples of Lord Maitreya. The others are nameless. I will be directed to appropriate books to read and study because it is important not to allow distractions. Other books will cloud my thinking.

I was asked to look closely at Kuthumi and report on what I saw. He appeared as a good-looking guy with piercing blue eyes and dark hair. He asked me to look at him again. This time I noticed he had black eyes, and the next time brown eyes. He said he had no need of form, and nor did the other disciples. It is only humans who need form in order to believe. He can be any form I conceive in my mind. It is only my perception of what is, and not the truth of reality. All that I see is my perception. As my perception changes, my truth and reality change.

Day three of my training on perception: Kuthumi said that all I see is my personal perception. Everyone sees something different according to personal perception. Other dimensions are available to be seen yet perception clouds this. A baby is born able to perceive many different dimensions simultaneously. They see light and colours. When a newly born baby looks into another's eyes and sees and feels a soul connection the baby is recognizing the other's soul by its light and energetic emanation. It takes some time for the baby to close down from its wider perceptual vision to see only the 3D world. Kuthumi said that I had integrated this training well.

A day or so later I received more instruction as: I need to learn to allow time to expand rather than try and control it, as control is the 3D approach. Control is connected to force and comes from the ego. Relaxing into task and trusting it to proceed within universal flow enables time to expand. I was told that I would be tested later so need to integrate this information.

I was tested – in 2011. I forced myself to write a technical astrology book because I'd been asked by my students and friend to do so. I created inflammation in my fingers through my negative thoughts of believing that I had to complete the task within a certain time. I tried to control and force the book into manifestation and lacked trust in the relaxed process. Each time I had a negative thought, or felt frustrated, my index finger would pain. All my fingers became very swollen. As the book neared completion I was finding it even more difficult to type. I decided to tune into my body's messages and learn from them. The main message was that I needed to relax into, and enjoy, the writing process rather then forcing it through ego control. Whoops! Where had all my spiritual training on trust gone?

I ceased writing for one week, and then, when I resumed, relaxed into the writing process. The pain ceased and, nine months later, the swelling had gone.

During another meditation Lord Maitreya said that I would be receiving messages from Kuthumi daily, through dreams and telepathy, and needed to make them concrete by writing them in my journal.

In early August Archangels Uriel and Gabriel took me once again into outer space where I was asked to view the solar system and to look at it very closely. I observed the planets in their fixed orbit and noticed the Sun giving out such a huge force that I could see energy waves rolling from it. The waves were very strong, almost seeming to have form. They appeared to be buffeting the planets yet the planets held their positions. It seemed the force emanating from the Sun could become so great it could blast a planet off its gravitational orbit. I realized that our precious planet Earth could be one to experience this catastrophic cosmic chaos. I was asked to ponder upon this and allow answers to emerge. Then I was taken to the Spiritual CEO's who thanked me for making the time available for contact and asked me to tune in again soon.

One answer emerged while editing this paragraph. In astrology, the Sun symbolically represents Spirit. Spiritual (solar) waves are bombarding our Earth with ever-increasing force encouraging humanity to "wake-up" to the truth that we are all One, and to act accordingly. If we do not change our collective consciousness then the huge force of the Sun could blast us off our orbit.

To add fuel to this perspective an article by Robert M. Schoch, PhD, in an alternative science magazine, Nexus (February/March 2013), explains how an early and forgotten civilization collapsed at the end of the last ice age when Earth experienced dramatic and cataclysmic changes. The article said how the Sun, from an astrophysical and geological perspective, continually churns out and, from time to time, spews massive solar storms. These storms left their mark in prehistoric records. From my remote viewing perspective I saw how this could have occurred, and how it's likely to occur again. The Atlantis continent is one that experienced a catastrophe and apparently geological records indicate the same timing as mentioned in the article. It is my understanding this timing occurred during the Age of Leo, the opposite zodiacal sign to Aquarius, approximately twelve thousand years ago during, or before, the last ice age.

We are experiencing a New Age - the Age of Aquarius - and historic themes repeat. Will we 'get it' this time around?

Frequencies of Energy

A few days later I received more of Kuthumi's training. He asked me to understand, and integrate, that all is energy vibrating at different frequencies. Matter and form are energy vibrating at a low or dense frequency. I was asked to imagine sawing through a piece of wood to make a table. The atoms in the cells of the wood 'scream' as they are split by the violence of the saw. A new form is created from the seeming 'death' of the old form.

"At present in your world the mass consciousness is being 'sawed' in order for a new form to take shape. It is so important to live in love, laughter, fun, and play as this creates a higher frequency which 'saw's through dense vibratory patterns. Call upon us for assistance. As we vibrate at a higher frequency we can charge you up bringing an input of higher voltage. We are available yet need to be asked. When you ask, maintain your focus and attention on the energy transference. We can bring light to dense energy patterns. Call upon us daily to aid your ascension process. The more light each one carries the more light is spread."

Energetic Density

Another transmission was received from Kuthumi a few days later:

"When humans incarnate into form upon the 3D earth plane a change occurs to their consciousness. 3D denseness envelops the energy field, which in turn reaches into those denser energy patterns of a specific nature that the soul has chosen to work with during the life. The hard aspects in the birth chart depict this dense patterning. There are many clues to this dense patterning carried in the energy field from previous existences. It is simply blocked energy. The goal of the soul is to clear the dense patterning in order to create a greater lightness of being, so it chooses an earthly sojourn to work towards its goal.

All is energy, vibrating at different frequencies.

A lighter frequency results from becoming conscious of, and fully understanding and integrating, the information contained within the blockages and then using the energy constructively. Once integrated, the etheric cellular memory re-adjusts and energy can then flow freely. Illumination has occurred. The 'lights are on' in the consciousness. It is simple.

We on the finer vibratory planes of existence do not encounter the density of energy that humans do. We offer our assistance yet we need to be asked. Our role is to provide a higher frequency to souls who ask. When a higher frequency develops within the human then a higher frequency is attracted. Circumstances change as the new level is accessed.

Love is the highest frequency. When operating from this place only high frequency is attracted. It is so."

Preparing to Fly

In my 3D life I was preparing to travel to USA alone. Kuthumi said I was to prepare for the greatest adventure of my life, and that all I had to do was to travel with absolute faith and trust, be spontaneous and follow my inner prompts and guidance. The adventure would begin as soon as I stepped on the plane at Cairns in north Queensland and I was to allow, and follow, my excitement.

During meditation on August 31st I decided to travel into the centre of my birth chart and invoke a planet to come to me. Saturn came, appearing very formal. He opened special doors saying they were the Pearly Gates and invited me to walk through into the unknown. I did so, without hesitation. It was incredibly light with the feeling of no-thing-ness. I felt totally at peace. Then he asked me to take on the energy of authority, as it was time to adopt this necessary quality.

So I decided to assert my authority to invoke my spiritual guides, who were with me instantly, explaining again that we are all one. I am part of them and they are part of me. We are all cells in the One, each one of us vibrating differently according to our individuality. They placed a crown of white lilies on my head and around my ankles so my feet were enveloped in the energy. The white lilies symbolized purity. They robed me in a white gown and I felt like a female warrior, beautiful, feminine yet strong. And then I experienced growing enormous wings.

USA Adventure

Days later during meditation, Kuthumi told me that my forthcoming trip to USA would be the most important trip of my entire life and that: "Everything is in readiness and every day will be beautiful". He said I would need three weeks away and requested I 'tune in' several times a day, and recommended I take with me some of my Young Living essential healing oils, flower essences and special crystals. And, he said, it was important to keep my heart chakra open and daily create feelings of love, as this would keep my frequency high. I was given a sceptre to signify I have become an authority of wisdom, and a cup to represent the Holy Grail.

In early September I travelled to USA to promote my books, including the three astrology books I'd written. These books started out as notes for my students and became workbooks.

It was the time of the 2000 Olympic games in Australia. Most of my family were attending the Sydney games however I apparently had my own Olympics to experience. I had been asked by Kuthumi to allow him to guide my actions while in USA and all I had to do was listen to, and act upon, my inner prompts. I particularly wanted to visit Sedona, situated near Phoenix in Arizona. I only had one contact in this state, an astrologer in Phoenix, however I totally trusted that all would work out. I flew into Phoenix and can remember waiting in my motel room for guidance on where to go and who to contact, for hours. When it came I immediately acted upon it. I spent the entire three weeks of my adventure waiting patiently for guidance and then acting upon it.

I liked being in Phoenix. My hotel room was large and

comfortable and a health food store was around the corner. I also enjoyed the symbolism of the name 'Phoenix'. The phoenix is the mythical bird that arises out of the ashes of the former self and is the third symbol for Scorpio. I felt I was that bird. Kuthumi said that this trip was an inner journey to access a place in my soul I had not yet accessed.

My meditation training on September 13th consisted of the Spiritual CEO's placing me in the centre of their circle and imbuing me with their high vibrational energy. They told me that each human cell carries psychological density. Matter, such as a table, is simply a collection of dense cells. When human cells become lighter, through developing self-awareness, higher consciousness and divine love, we can move through the denseness of matter. This, they said, is the process of evolution.

During my few days in Phoenix I was introduced to the local branch of the American Federation of Astrologers who invited me to join their organization and attend their conference the following year to present my work. I was also invited to address a large class at an astrology school. We had a great time and they purchased my trilogy of astrology books for their student's library.

En route by shuttle bus to Sedona, a few hours drive from Phoenix, I felt memories stirring from another time and place, and wondered what adventures awaited me. The opening ceremony for the Olympic games in Sydney was shown on USA TV that night and I was fortunate to be able to view some of it from my motel room, situated near the airport vortex.

The next morning I went for an early morning walk, as was my custom in Australia. I wanted to explore the airport vortex area before sunrise and, after walking along a well-trodden hiking trail for some time, decided to sit and relax on a red rock overlooking a majestic and awe-inspiring valley of red rock formations. The country is very much like the colour of Australia's red centre, and the rock formations are also similar. I felt completely at home and closed my eyes to begin a meditation of gratitude. Immediately the Spirit of the Sedona land came to me asking if I would be willing to do healing work for Mother Earth. She said that I naturally work in other dimensions and needed to come to Sedona to do some of that other dimensional work. However, she said, her request was specifically for Mother Earth. I agreed. She said she would guide me and all I had to do was to follow my impulses that would be guided by her prompts. Then she adjusted my frequency by using her healing hands to brush my aura.

I felt a deep emotion of gratitude and love for the area, and its incredible beauty, and felt equally as nourished here as I did in the Andean mountains of Peru. Is this ancient Lemurian energy? I asked myself. I felt that it was. Lemuria was an ancient continent, now far below the Pacific Ocean and the beings lived predominantly a spiritual life deeply connected to Mother Nature.

At 6.00am the next day I again walked to the airport vortex and was guided to hike to a special spot, exactly opposite Bell Rock. I was shown when and where to stop. I did a sunrise ritual standing to face the magnificent sunrise, imagining the rays entering my 3rd eye chakra. Then I turned and invoked the Sun's rays to enter each of the chakras along my spine. When I sat down to meditate the Spirit of Sedona came again and told me a little of my history there. She spoke of a time when I had been an Indian Prince, in training to be the Chief, however an incident occurred and I was not able to adopt that role. I was a strong, fearless warrior with a heart full of love and a soul filled with wisdom, very connected to the Earth and stars. I felt her story deeply resonate in my body so knew it to be true. It explained why I knew, on a soul level, all the exercises that were given at the psychologist's workshop in Santa Fe years ago.

Apparently I had come back to this area to re-capture the energy of that fine man. She asked if I would return to the same spot at the same time during the next two days. I agreed, feeling balanced and happy to serve.

The next morning, when walking again to the airport vortex trail, the Spirit of Sedona appeared to me. At a specific spot on my walk she asked me to create a light funnel through which trapped souls could exit. I happily did the healing procedure she outlined and observed many souls leaving to go to the light. There seemed to be thousands of them. As I was sitting in that awesome place I reflected upon my many trips overseas and realized that the times I travelled to the mountains were the ones where I experienced the greatest uplifting and enlightening experiences. I was then shown how the Earth could be viewed as an astrological mandala with energy lines running between various energetic vortices. Sedona was obviously a place where vortices connected because the energy was so balanced.

My next town to visit was Denver situated in the mile high mountains of Colorado. It was the Equinox, September 21st, a time when the Earth is perfectly balanced. I have demonstrated this perfect balance to many students by showing them how to place a fresh egg on a flat table and have it stay there completely balanced and without aid. Why not try it for yourself?

During the flight I experienced clear contact with

Kuthumi who said there were many pockets of darkness in the Denver area and my work involved bringing light into that darkness. He recommended I stay in a state of love, trust, faith and light and do my best to be fully in the present. He also recommended I drink plenty of clean water. He showed me how the Spiritual CEO's are energy without form existing in timeless space. There are no structures and their 'wings' are simply huge auras.

A few days later I was offered a wonderful opportunity to experience, and understand, how I allow my power base of love to erode and then instantly become drained of energy. When in this weakened state I attracted a head cold. I could see very clearly the exact moment when and how this weakness occurred. I corrected and spoke my truth, with dignity and authority, to my 3D 'teacher'. I felt empowered and knew the cold would immediately go away. It did.

I had awakened to my powerless game, saw what I needed to see, accepted responsibility and acted constructively. This was part of the inner spiritual transformational work I was called to Denver to do. As one individual transforms dark energy patterns into light through the light of conscious self-understanding, and by taking immediate constructive action, the resultant lighter energy shines in the individual's aura and then touches those within its field of influence. This is an energetic way that transformation and regeneration of the human race takes place.

As part of my return trip home to Australia I had another stop over at Guam. Kuthumi said I had work to do there and to simply follow my impulses. I was driven to a former war zone and felt sick in my stomach as I picked up on the density and darkness of previous violent warring acts. I did a great deal of spiritual cleansing until the area cleared of psychic contamination.

I returned home to Australia on the day the Sydney Olympic games ended.

A "Walk-In" Experience

A woman emerged from the ether
A smile dancing on her lips
Her skin was luminous, ethereal,
Who was she?
Was she from another time, or dimension?
As the mists of time dissolved
The face of the woman became clear
And sparkled with luminosity
A heart shaped ring of red flowers encircled her head
She had a presence, a quality
Divine love emanating from her being
Who was She?
Where did she come from?
Was she from another time, or dimension?
Was she Venus, Aphrodite?
A woman emerged from the ethers
A smile dancing on her lips
Her skin was luminous, ethereal,
Her eyes were pools of endless light.
Her robe was silver, floating around her body
Giving her an air of softness and delicacy.
Who was She?
Where did she come from?
Was she from another time or dimension?
"Can you enlighten me? I ask,
"Are you an aspect of me?

Are you a representation of my Higher Self"?
Will the answer come?
The woman of luminosity asked that I travel with her
into her world to discover her secrets and message.
One dimension merged into another as we
joined together in the universal dance.
The woman of luminosity and I were one.

The third momentous experience of this year occurred on October 2nd 2000. My 3D life is relatively normal and I am essentially a practical person. Regardless of my starry and celestial experiences I simply get on with the day-to-day jobs at hand.

As mentioned earlier I'm often called upon to rest after lunch in order to participate in spiritual service work. I would feel this strong pull to rest, even though I didn't feel tired. Then I would drift into mediation, be taken somewhere to do the work, return and resume my 3D life. I never questioned this calling. Sometimes I was conscious of the service work I was involved in and sometimes not. I didn't need to know.

After lunch this day I felt an overpowering need to rest on my bed. Completely relaxed I drifted into an altered state. Again I experienced the most amazing energy expansion within me. It was similar to the recent Jupiter/Uranus experience.

I felt as if my energy field became so large it encompassed the entire universe. Fully conscious and alert I nestled into this expanded state of awareness, observing myself in the experience. I saw that I was one with a myriad of stars and we were a mass of vibrating energy. My energy field expanded even further until I felt I was infinite, without beginning and without end. I was a no-thing, without form, in a state where there were no boundaries and no limitations. This state of cosmic bliss expanded yet again to a place where there was no sound or motion. I experienced pure stillness and ecstasy, and knew I was one with Source.

Time stood still as this state of bliss expanded again. Then I observed the Spiritual Hierarchy gathering around me, along with masses of other ethereal light beings. I became aware that a joyous celebration was about to take place. I was asked to stand in front of the spokesperson whereupon I was awarded a gold medal for the soul work I had done. There was much applause. I received tremendous love and respect from the assembled gathering.

From high above I saw a bright light descend, an etheric substance in the shape of a light being. Then I observed an etheric light substance ascend from my body. It was the soul/spirit essence of Barbara ascending to a higher dimensional plane of existence while simultaneously Ashtara's soul/spirit essence descended to take her place. It appeared as if they were passing each other in a cosmic elevator. I clearly felt the different energy and essence of Ashtara enter my body.

Ashtara 'walked in' to a perfectly healthy, aware and conscious human being.

I, the observer of the experience, was told that Barbara had fulfilled her incarnational purpose and had gone on to experience other realms. It had been her final incarnation on Earth and it may well be Ashtara's. Ashtara has an issue with recognition and approval that Barbara did not have and her real work could only begin when this issue has been totally healed through the transmutation process.

Symbolically the exchange had to take place after

the Olympic games. Olympic athletes receive medals for endurance, discipline, persistence, effort and will. Barbara received her medal for demonstrating these qualities on her journey to ascension and the attainment of Christ consciousness. She left in a blaze of Olympic glory having accomplished all she set out to do, with honour, integrity and love.

And now it was Ashtara's turn.

Author's Note

I hope you enjoyed my story. I have much more to share and will do so in the sequel to this book, *The Magdalen Codes*. In it you will find answers to many questions you might have such as: Why did Mary Magdalen choose to show herself to me when I was about to study advanced evolutionary astrology, and what was my karmic duty associated with the sacred circle dance Paneurythmy? I intend to begin writing the sequel in 2013 but for now I invite you to visit:

www.IAmAnExperiment.com

Blessings and love,
Ashtara

ABOUT THE AUTHOR

Ashtara is a professional astrologer, metaphysician, educator and author of ten books. She is an inspiring and entertaining speaker in the field of human consciousness, spirituality, metaphysics and holistic health presenting her work nationally and internationally. Her books, C.D's teaching and published articles inspire and motivate thousands of people globally.

She is dedicated to awakening, and empowering, people to access higher states of consciousness that enable spiritual enlightenment and optimum health through mind/ body/spirit union.

Her in-depth Astrological Analysis of your birth chart is available through her website.

www.ashtara.com

Journey with *Ashtara* to Divine Love and Light

"My heart is open and I trust my inner guidance"

Ashtara lives by, and shares this affirmation because it helped to open her heart to ecstatic experiences of divine love.

"My mind is open and I willingly allow expansion by listening to my intuition and heart-felt spiritual guidance"

This affirmation assisted Ashtara in opening incredible doorways in her mind that are so far untapped by science. She offers it with a prayer that you too will experience loving mind-expansion and higher perceptions.

Ashtara invites you to enjoy some of the valuable goodies she offers at
www.IAmAnExperiment.com

- ♥ Life enhancing affirmations and exercises
- ♥ Behind-the-scenes articles
- ♥ Special frequency raising meditations
- ♥ Answers to many life questions
- ♥ Regular newsletters
- ♥ A family of like-minded friends

Make **www.IAmAnExperiment.com** your cyber home and join with a global family of like-minded friends who share similar experiences.

Join Us on Facebook **www.Facebook.com/IAmAnExperiment**

www.ingramcontent.com/pod-product-compliance
Lightning Source LLC
Chambersburg PA
CBHW031242290426
44109CB00012B/396